W9-ADM-958

AMERICAN NURSES
ASSOCIATION

Scope AND
Standards
OF PRACTICE

Addictions
Nursing

American Nurses Association
Silver Spring, Maryland
2013

S/14
Direct
$29.95

American Nurses Association
8515 Georgia Avenue, Suite 400
Silver Spring, MD 20910-3492
1-800-274-4ANA
http://www.NursingWorld.org

Published by Nursesbooks.org
The Publishing Program of ANA
http://www.Nursesbooks.org/

The International Nurses Society on Addictions (IntSNA) and the American Nurses Association (ANA) are national professional associations. This joint IntSNA—ANA publication—*Addictions Nursing: Scope and Standards of Practice*—reflects the thinking of the practice specialty of addictions nursing on various issues and should be reviewed in conjunction with state board of nursing policies and practices. State law, rules, and regulations govern the practice of nursing, while *Addictions Nursing: Scope and Standards of Practice* guides addictions nurses in the application of their professional skills and responsibilities.

The International Nurses Society on Addictions (IntSNA) is a professional nursing specialty organization founded in 1975.

IntSNA's mission is to advance excellence in nursing care for the prevention and treatment of addictions for diverse populations across all practice settings through advocacy, collaboration, education, research and policy development. The goal of IntNSA is to help nurses provide comprehensive, high-quality nursing care for addicted patients and their families.

IntNSA's members are committed to the prevention, intervention, treatment, and management of addictive disorders including alcohol and other drug dependencies, nicotine dependencies, eating disorders, dual and multiple diagnosis, and process addictions such as gambling.

The American Nurses Association is the only full-service professional organization representing the interests of the nation's 3.1 million registered nurses through its constituent/state nurses associations and its organizational affiliates. The ANA advances the nursing profession by fostering high standards of nursing practice, promoting the rights of nurses in the workplace, projecting a positive and realistic view of nursing, and by lobbying the Congress and regulatory agencies on healthcare issues affecting nurses and the public.

ISBN-13: 978-1-55810-526-3   SAN: 851-3481   10/2013

First printing: October 2013

Contents

Contributors

Editors

Deborah S. Finnell, DNS, PMHNP-BC, CARN-AP, FAAN

Karen Allen, PhD, RN, FAAN

Writing Work Group Members

Lauren Broyles, PhD, RN

Colleen Corte, PhD, RN

Deborah S. Finnell, DNS, PMHNP-BC, CARN-AP, FAAN

Katherine S. Fornili, MPH, RN, CARN

Dana Murphy-Parker, MS, PMHNP-BC

Christine Savage, PhD, RN, CARN, FAAN

Stephen Strobbe, PhD, RN, NP, PMHNP-BC, CARN-AP

ANA Staff

Carol J. Bickford, PhD, RN-BC, CPHIMS – Content editor

Maureen E. Cones, Esq. – Legal counsel

Yvonne Daley Humes, MSA – Project coordinator

Eric Wurzbacher, BA – Project editor

About the International Nurses Society on Addictions

The International Nurses Society on Addictions Nurses Society on Addictions (IntSNA) is a professional specialty organization founded in 1975 for nurses committed to the prevention, intervention, treatment, and management of addictive disorders including alcohol and other drug dependencies, nicotine dependencies, eating disorders, dual and multiple diagnosis, and process addictions such as gambling.

The IntSNA mission is to advance excellence in nursing care for the prevention and treatment of addictions for diverse populations across all practice settings through advocacy, collaboration, education, research and policy development.

The goal of IntNSA is to help nurses provide comprehensive, high-quality nursing care for addicted patients and their families.

About the American Nurses Association

The American Nurses Association (ANA) is the only full-service professional organization representing the interests of the nation's 3.1 million registered nurses through its constituent/state nurses associations and its organizational affiliates. The ANA advances the nursing profession by fostering high standards of nursing practice, promoting the rights of nurses in the workplace, projecting a positive and realistic view of nursing, and by lobbying the Congress and regulatory agencies on health care issues affecting nurses and the public.

About Nursesbooks.org, The Publishing Program of ANA

Nursesbooks.org publishes books on ANA core issues and programs, including ethics, leadership, quality, specialty practice, advanced practice, and the profession's enduring legacy. Best known for the foundational documents of the profession on nursing ethics, scope and standards of practice, and social policy, Nursesbooks.org is the publisher for the professional, career-oriented nurse, reaching and serving nurse educators, administrators, managers, and researchers as well as staff nurses in the course of their professional development.

Introduction

Addictions nursing is defined as the protection, promotion, and optimization of health and abilities for individuals, families, communities, and populations affected by alcohol, tobacco, and other drug use and persistent and recurrent maladaptive behaviors. Addictions nursing spans the continuum of substance use and behaviors that can become persistent and maladaptive, leading to substance use and addictive disorders.

Addictions nurses utilize a holistic framework, recognizing the biological, psychological, social, and spiritual factors associated with and affected by substance use and related maladaptive behaviors. This framework provides an integral approach to substance use and addictive disorders, consistent with the complex interactions that occur within the body-brain-mind-emotions-spirit-environment. Despite decades of research related to the neurobiological under-pinnings of addictions, a moral paradigm persists. Addictions nurses challenge negative attitudes and beliefs about addictions through the dissemination of evidence-based knowledge to current and future nurses and other healthcare providers, patients, and the public.

Consistent with the American Nurses Association definition of nursing (ANA, 2010b), addictions nursing encompasses the four essential characteristics of nursing: human responses or phenomena, theory application, nursing actions or interventions, and outcomes. Addictions nursing focuses on the prevention of illness and injury; alleviation of suffering through the diagnosis and treatment of associated human responses; and advocacy in the care of individuals, families, communities, and populations affected by alcohol, tobacco, and other drug use and maladaptive behaviors that may become addictive disorders.

Addictions nursing has been recognized as a specialty for 30 years. Emerging from this recognition were publications on nursing practice (American Nurses Association, National Nurses Society on Addiction, & Drug and Alcohol Nurses Association, 1987), standards of addictions nursing (National Nurses Society on Addictions & American Nurses Association, 1989), and the *Scope and Standards of Addictions Nursing Practice* (ANA & IntNSA, 2004). The International Nurses Society on Addictions (IntNSA; formerly the National Nurses Society on Addictions) is a professional specialty organization for nurses committed to the prevention, intervention, treatment, and management of addictive disorders, including alcohol and other drug dependencies, as well as eating disorders, dual and multiple diagnoses, and other addictions such as gambling. With an increased emphasis on prevention and treatment of substance use and addictive disorders, IntNSA's mission is *to advance excellence in nursing care for the prevention and treatment of addictions for diverse populations across all practice settings through advocacy, collaboration, education, research, and policy development (http://www.intnsa.org).*

Addictions Nursing: Scope and Standards of Practice outlines the expectations of the professional role within which all registered nurses specializing in the prevention and treatment of substance use and addictive disorders should practice. The term *addictions nurse* used in this document reflects this broad range of practice and is not restricted to the treatment of those with a substance use or addictive disorder. Building upon a sound base as a registered nurse, the nurse specializing in addictions has additional knowledge and skills related to substance use and addictive disorders.

The foundation and framework for the specialty scope and standards are informed by three documents of the American Nurses Association (ANA):

- *Nursing's Social Policy Statement: The Essence of the Profession* (ANA, 2010b). This document describes professional nursing's accountability to the public and identifies the processes of self-regulation, professional regulation, and legal regulation as mechanisms to maintain public trust.

- *Code of Ethics for Nurses with Interpretive Statements* (ANA, 2001). This document provides significant guidance for all nurses and their nursing practice in every setting.

- *Nursing: Scope and Standards of Practice, Second Edition* (ANA, 2010a). This document defines the scope and standards of practice for all registered nurses, including the advanced practice registered nurse (APRN). This document served as a template for delineating the details and complexity of the addictions nursing specialty, and for describing what this nursing specialty is, what specialty nurses do, and the responsibilities for which specialty nurses are accountable. The scope and standards of nursing practice are highly valued by registered nurses nationally and internationally and are regularly referenced by those engaged in legal, regulatory, administrative, educational, and research activities.

The primary audience of this professional resource includes registered nurses of any educational level and employed in any setting who serve individuals of any age affected by substance use and related behaviors that can become persistent and maladaptive. This scope and standards document will be a reference source for legislators, regulators, legal counsel, and the judicial system. Agencies, organizations, nurse administrators, other nurses not working in this specialty, and other interprofessional colleagues will find this an invaluable reference. In addition, persons with actual or potential substance use and addictive disorders, their family/legal guardians, communities, and populations using healthcare and nursing services can use this document to better understand the role and responsibilities of registered nurses and advanced practice registered nurses who specialize in the prevention, intervention, treatment, and recovery of individuals, families, and populations affected by substance use and addictive disorders.

Scope of Practice of Addictions Nursing

Overview of Addictions Nursing

The Institute of Medicine (IOM) report, *The Future of Nursing: Leading Change, Advancing Health* (IOM, 2011), has been a catalyst for advancement of the nursing profession and patient-centered care. Nurses specializing in addictions are in prime positions to lead change in the delivery of health care for individuals, families, communities, and populations affected by substance use and maladaptive behaviors. Practicing to the full extent of their education and training, these specialty nurses are at the vanguard of care provision across the continuum of substance use and addictive disorders. Nurses are educated to view patients holistically within the context of the family and the community. Because nurses are often the first healthcare providers that patients encounter, nurses are in ideal roles to detect substance use and maladaptive behaviors. This first contact with patients highlights the value of a specialist in addictions nursing. After identifying the at-risk person, the addictions nurse can seamlessly move to the assessment phase of the nursing process with the goal of preventing progression along the continuum or otherwise intervening to minimize the associated consequences of the substance use or maladaptive behaviors.

Addictions nurses serve as advocates not only for their individual patients, but also for the implementation of policies and programs that can reduce the harm associated with substance use and maladaptive behaviors. In this way, addictions nurses provide the leadership needed to align nursing with the global efforts included in the World Health Organization (WHO) publication (Blas & Kurup, 2010) that emphasizes the need for nations to implement effective upstream prevention, with a focus on those experiencing health inequities associated with substance use.

Substance use and addictive disorders are evident across the lifespan, settings, genders, cultures, and special populations. This specialty nursing role commands knowledge of the fundamental biological, behavioral, environmental, psychological, social, cultural, and spiritual aspects of human responses to the use of substances and engagement in behaviors that can lead to addictive disorders. The registered nurse specializing in the prevention and treatment of substance use and addictive disorders has an essential and integral role in promoting access to care and delivery of evidence-based interventions to prevent the onset of, or progression to, substance use and addictive disorders.

Screening, Brief Intervention, and Referral to Treatment (SBIRT)

All registered nurses should have the requisite knowledge and competencies needed for screening, brief intervention, and referral to treatment (SBIRT) in order to identify and effectively respond to alcohol use and related disorders (Strobbe, Perhats, & Broyles, in press). SBIRT is a set of clinical strategies widely recommended for improving the identification and management of unhealthy alcohol use and tobacco use. A publication from the National Institute on Alcohol Abuse and Alcoholism (NIAAA), *Helping Patients Who Drink Too Much: A Clinician's Guide* (NIAAA, 2007), is an excellent resource for nurses and other healthcare providers and is easily accessible at http://www.niaaa.nih.gov/guide.

Routine screening and brief intervention are evidence-based approaches with alcohol and tobacco users to prevent progression to abuse and dependence and other consequences (American College of Surgeons Committee on Trauma, 2006; Committee on Health Care for Underserved Women, 2011; Higgins-Biddle, Hungeford, & Cates-Wessel, 2009; Department of Veterans Affairs, 2009; Sullivan & Fleming, 1997; U.S. Preventive Services Task Force, 2004). Screening determines the extent of alcohol and tobacco use and may reveal a need for additional assessment and interventions.

Brief intervention is keenly aligned with a harm-reduction approach. Harm reduction is a pragmatic approach to reduce the harmful consequences of alcohol and drug use or other high-risk activities by incorporating several strategies that cut across the spectrum from safer use to managed use to abstinence. The primary goal of most harm-reduction approaches is to meet individuals "where they are at" and, rather than ignoring or condemning the harmful behaviors, working with the individual or community to minimize the harmful effects of a given behavior (Marlatt & Witkiewitz, 2010). Harmful substance use consists of a pattern of psychoactive substance use that is causing damage to health.

The damage may be physical (e.g., hepatitis following injection of drugs) or mental (e.g., depressive episodes secondary to heavy alcohol intake). Harmful use commonly, but not invariably, has adverse social consequences; however, social consequences by themselves are not sufficient to justify a diagnosis of harmful use (WHO, 2011b).

Brief intervention is a nonconfrontational, patient-centered approach to unhealthy alcohol and tobacco use. Taking the form of a 5- to 15-minute semi-structured motivational discussion, brief intervention is intended to raise awareness of alcohol- or smoking-related consequences and motivate a patient toward behavior change (i.e., reduction in or cessation of use). Brief intervention typically involves the use of motivational interviewing techniques. These techniques include expressing empathy through reflective listening, developing cognitive discrepancy between clients' goals or values and their current behaviors, avoidance of argument and direct confrontation, adjusting to client resistance rather than opposing it directly, and supporting self-efficacy and optimism (Miller & Rollnick, 2002). These techniques are clearly consistent with professional nursing practice.

Referral to treatment is provided to patients who need more extensive substance-related treatment. Support and treatment can be provided through referral to specialty care, such as detoxification services, outpatient counseling, and self-help groups (Sullivan & Fleming, 1997).

The escalating illicit drug and prescription drug misuse in the United States commands attention of all registered nurses. In 2011, 3.1 million persons aged 12 or older reported a first-time illicit drug use and 6.1 million persons aged 12 or older reported the nonmedical use of prescription psychotherapeutic drugs in the past month (Substance Abuse and Mental Health Services Administration [SAMHSA], 2012). Though there is currently insufficient evidence to determine the benefits and harms of screening for illicit drug use (U.S. Preventive Services Task Force, 2008), the publication by the National Institute on Drug Abuse (NIDA), *Screening for Drug Use in General Medical Settings* (NIDA, 2012), is a resource to assist clinicians serving adult patients in screening for drug use. SBIRT is consistent with and incorporates the "5 As": Ask, Advise, Assess, Assist, Arrange follow-up (Fiore, Bailey, Cohen, Dorfman, & Goldstein, 2000). NIDA provides a portfolio of resources to help nurses better address drug abuse among their patients (see http://www.drugabuse.gov/nidamed-medical-health-professionals). The portfolio includes information on SBIRT, in addition to providing patient materials and curriculum resources.

Continuum of Substance Use and Addictive Disorders: Nursing Foci

PREVENTION

Prevention efforts related to substance use and health consequences have shifted over the past 20 years, from a narrow focus on the end of the continuum of use and dependence to a broader focus that includes the continuum of use across the lifespan. The Healthy People 2020 objectives related to substance use (U.S. Department of Health and Human Services [U.S. DHHS], 2011) and the World Health Organization's report on alcohol reflect this shift (Blas & Kurup, 2010). The focus is on the reduction in harm associated with substance use or engagement in potentially addictive behaviors across the spectrum of prevention, rather than taking a downstream approach and focusing on treatment alone.

Nursing expertise in addictions is essential because nurses are the largest segment of the healthcare workforce and are often the first healthcare providers to interact with individuals and families seeking care. The Savage and Finnell Conceptual Model of the Continuum of Substance Use and Maladaptive Behaviors: Nursing Foci© is a useful conceptual model for guiding nursing assessment, diagnosis, outcomes identification, planning, implementation, and evaluation along the continuum of substance use and addictive disorders (see Figure 1; see Appendix B for a larger version). Three levels of prevention are applied across this continuum:

- *Primary prevention*: Specific practices for the prevention of a disorder in susceptible individuals or populations; population-based *health promotion* efforts aimed at reducing both the incidence and prevalence of the disease. For example, individuals with presymptomatic or unrecognized symptomatic alcohol and other drug use can be identified through *screening* for alcohol and other drug use, irrespective of the risk status of the individual.

- *Secondary prevention*: Interventions provided when a problem is in the early stages (e.g., alcohol consumption above recommended limits) before significant morbidity occurs. *Advise and assist brief interventions* (NIAAA, 2007) are used to raise awareness about the problem and motivate individuals to adopt healthy behavior (e.g., reduce alcohol consumption, abstain from drug use, cease gambling activities). The goal is to promote health behaviors noted at the beginning of the continuum. Yet, for some, treatment for the acute phase may be warranted, and thus *referral to specialty treatment* is recommended.

- *Tertiary prevention*: Directed toward preventing damage, slowing the progression, preventing complications, providing effective treatments, and helping restore individuals to a healthy state (i.e., **recovery**).

FIGURE 1. **The Savage and Finnell Conceptual Model of the Continuum of Substance Use and Maladaptive Behaviors: Nursing Foci**©

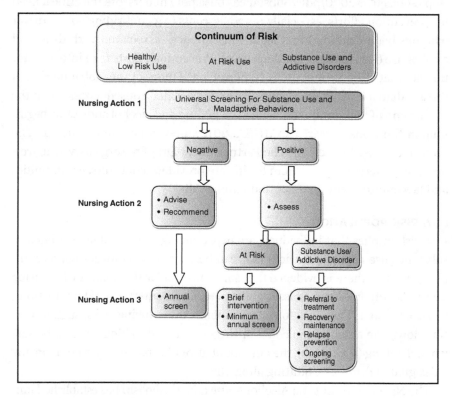

In any 12-month period, about 47% of the U.S. adult population may have a substance use disorder or addictive disorder with serious negative consequences (Sussman, Lisha, & Griffiths, 2011). This means that more than half the population may be not be using substances or engaging in behaviors that are maladaptive; or, if using substances or engaging in maladaptive behaviors, not doing so at the

---

Legend: Substance use (alcohol, tobacco, and other drugs) and behaviors that are maladaptive can progress to substance use and addictive disorders. The *level of risk* is identified by using established screening tools. Individuals with detectable risk are further assessed for clinically significant impairment or distress. The gradual shading in the figure conveys the progression from healthy risk or low risk to at-risk to a diagnosable disorder. *Nursing actions* are tailored according to the level or risk and in accord with guidelines for brief intervention and referral to treatment. Taking the level of risk into account, the overarching clinical outcomes focus on reducing risk associated with substance use and maladaptive behaviors. Across all levels of risk, nurses engage in patient-centered discussions to negotiate goals fostering optimal clinical outcomes. Recognizing that substance use and maladaptive behaviors are not static, screening is repeated during subsequent encounters in accord with the individual's risk level.

degree to which there are recurrent and significant adverse consequences or where discontinuation of the substance or behavior may cause withdrawal symptoms.

Thus, efforts should be directed toward the majority of the population that is healthy, at low risk, or at risk, to prevent substance use and other addictive disorders. The Healthy People 2020 objectives (http://healthypeople.gov/2020 /topicsobjectives2020/pdfs/SubstanceAbuse.pdf) underscore the critical need for prevention efforts, especially for adolescents (e.g., not riding with a driver who has been drinking) and legal consequences associated with drug and alcohol use (e.g., ignition interlock laws). Prevention efforts take into account the fact that risky alcohol use is responsible for more of the global burden of disease than a level where alcohol use and associated consequences are at the further end of the continuum. With 90% of drug and alcohol addictions beginning in the teenage years (SAMHSA, 2012), prevention efforts such as The Medicine Abuse Project™ of The Partnership at DrugFree.org (www.drugfree. org) are garnering support from healthcare providers, educators, communities and law enforcement, parents, and families alike.

LOW-RISK POPULATION

Low risk implies that individuals are experiencing some problems related to substance use and/or behaviors that can become maladaptive, such as gambling. That is, there is evidence that substance use or the behavior is causing injury; health problems; or issues related to family, interpersonal interactions, work, or school. The focus for intervention is on reducing risks, such as cutting down the amount of alcohol or drug consumed, taking steps to be safe when drinking (e.g., pacing the amount of alcohol consumed per hour, having a designated driver), or quitting altogether.

The National Institute on Alcohol Abuse and Alcoholism has established limits for alcohol consumption beyond which is considered more than is medically safe. These amounts are based on a standard drink. A *standard drink* is any drink that contains about 0.6 fluid ounces or 14 grams of "pure" alcohol (e.g., 12 fluid ounces of regular beer, 8–9 fluid ounces of malt liquor, 5 fluid ounces of table wine, 1.5 fluid ounces of 80-proof liquor). Healthy adult men should have no more than 4 standard drinks on any day AND no more than 14 standard drinks per week; healthy adult women should have no more than 3 standard drinks on any day AND no more than 7 drinks per week (NIAAA, 2007).

AT-RISK POPULATION

The segment of the population considered at risk is generally seen in primary care settings where preventive or episodic health care is sought, emergency departments where an urgent medical problem or injuries are treated, or hospital settings where acute health needs are addressed. "At risk" does not mean "no risk." For example, alcohol consumption can cause both immediate health risks (e.g., unintentional injuries, miscarriage and stillbirth, alcohol poisoning) and long-term health risks (e.g., cardiovascular problems, liver diseases, neurological problems). The nonconfrontational, patient-centered approach of *brief intervention* can be effective in raising awareness of alcohol-related consequences and motivating a patient toward behavior change (Sullivan & Fleming, 1997). This brief intervention entails providing advice about the substance or behavior, assisting the patient in making a change (e.g., cutting down or quitting, pharmacological treatment), and arranging for specialty assessment and/or referring to specialty treatment as appropriate.

SUBSTANCE USE AND ADDICTIVE DISORDERS

Individuals who are detected to be at high risk because of alcohol and drug use (i.e., amount, frequency, pattern of use, consequences) and/or behaviors that are maladaptive need further assessment to determine the criteria associated with a substance use or addictive disorder. Criteria for diagnosis are specified in *Diagnostic and Statistical Manual* of the American Psychiatric Association (2013) and the World Health Organization's *International Statistical Classification of Diseases and Related Health Problems* (2004), both of which undergo periodic revision. Referral to specialty treatment is indicated for individuals at this end of the continuum so they can access medical detoxification and evidence-based addictions treatment, rehabilitation, and recovery services/support.

In summary, there is a critical need for *all* registered nurses to have the requisite knowledge and competencies to screen for at-risk substance use, assess for possible addictive disorders, and intervene accordingly, including referral to specialty treatment if indicated. There is also a need for addictions nurses with demonstrated advanced knowledge and competencies related to substance use and addictive disorders across the continuum and the lifespan. Addictions nurses are instrumental in translating evidence-based knowledge to practice, including disseminating that knowledge to their registered nurse colleagues in other specialties. Addictions nurses have the expertise to institute interventions across the continuum of use addressing prevention, early identification of and intervention with those who are at risk, and care of the individual with a substance use or addictive disorder.

The specialty nursing scope of practice statement provides a complete picture of the dynamic and complex practice of the nursing specialty and its evolving boundaries and membership. The profession of nursing has one scope of practice that encompasses the full range of nursing practice, pertinent to both general and specialty practice. This scope of addictions nursing describes the breadth and depth to which individual registered nurses engage in addictions nursing practice. The sections that follow describe *why* there is a need for addictions nursing, *who* addictions nurses are, *where* and *when* they practice, and *what* they do. Finally, the discussion on guiding principles and values provides the ethical context for *how* addictions nurses practice.

Context for Addictions Nursing

Substance use and addictive disorders are global phenomena with serious, costly, and profound implications in terms of biological, psychological, sociocultural, and spiritual health and illness for individuals, families, communities, and populations. These disorders can occur across the lifespan, from infancy through older adulthood, and contribute to increased rates of disability and premature death. Regardless of clinical setting or practice, nurses across the United States and around the world have the capacity to positively influence outcomes related to substance use and addictive disorders through expanded and energetic efforts directed toward prevention, intervention, and treatment.

The use of substances, particularly alcohol and tobacco, is a serious public health issue. Tobacco-related illnesses account for more than 5 million deaths per year worldwide, and tobacco use is the single most preventable cause of chronic disease and death (WHO, 2011b). Harmful use of alcohol accounts for 2.5 million fatalities every year, including 320,000 young people between 15 and 29 years of age, and is the third leading risk factor for poor health globally (WHO, 2011a). Often, tobacco use goes hand in hand with other substance use, with many who develop a substance use disorder meeting the criteria for both alcohol and drug dependence (NIAAA, 2008).

The Institute of Medicine (IOM) proposed a continuum-of-health framework in the 1990s that was adopted by the Substance Abuse and Mental Health Services Administration. The full model depicts a comprehensive continuum of care: prevention, treatment, and maintenance. The three prevention-level categories include universal, selected, and indicated interventions and have been widely adopted in the addictions field (Institute of Medicine Prevention Model, 1997, pp. 10–15; Nitzkin & Smith, 2004).

Universal prevention intervention occurs with the population as a whole, including those at risk and those not at risk. An example of this strategy is be a public service announcement or an education program delivered to all of the students in a school district. The whole population is the targeted recipient of interventions intended to prevent the potential health problem from occurring.

The selected level of intervention targets a subset of the population at increased level of risk for developing disease. The risk factors can include age, gender, genetic, environmental, and/or socioeconomic risk factors. For example, instead of delivering an anti-smoking educational program to the entire school district, the program may target males ages 11 to 14 who have family members who smoke. At this level of intervention, the target is everyone in a subgroup, regardless of individual risk.

Indicated interventions target populations with a high probability of developing disease that have early signs of the disorder or subclinical condition; for example, persons with risky or harmful alcohol use who do not meet criteria for an alcohol use disorder. The purpose is to prevent the development of a substance abuse disorder. This approach is widely used in the addictions field to develop programs for individuals who show early warning signs. In adolescents, this may include falling grades, binge drinking, or episodes of drinking and driving. This level of intervention requires a more intensive, often multilevel approach. The SAMHSA report gives multiple examples of interventions at each level (Institute of Medicine Prevention Model, 1997; Nitzkin & Smith, 2004).

Reduction in the burden of disease associated with substance use requires a healthcare workforce capable of implementing evidence-based interventions across the continuum of substance use and the lifespan. If healthcare workers understand the continuum of substance use, including adverse health consequences for both those who use and those who use substances and those who do not, the scope of prevention and intervention efforts is greatly expanded. Though use of some substances, such as alcohol and (increasingly) marijuana, is sometimes considered to be a socially acceptable and normative practice in the U. S., substance use adversely affects health across the lifespan, including but not limited to injury, cancer, hypertension, stroke, liver disease, and brain damage.

The likelihood that a nurse will come in contact with a person who consumes alcohol is high. In 2010, among Americans aged 12 or older, approximately

51.8% reported current alcohol use, 27.4% reported tobacco use, and 22.6% reported using illicit drugs (SAMHSA, 2011). The possible impact of having a knowledgeable and competent nursing workforce can be illustrated through the use of brief intervention for those who report heavy episodic drinking. If successful with a third of the patients they encountered with at-risk drinking, an estimated $10.4 billion could be saved in medical settings and $148.6 billion could be saved from a societal perspective due to reduced alcohol-related hospital emergency department visits, alcohol-related criminal events, and lost productivity related to alcohol use (Molander, Yonker, & Krahn, 2010).

Levels of Addictions Nurses

GENERALIST ADDICTIONS NURSES

At a minimum, a degree in an accredited prelicensure nursing program leading to eligibility to sit for the NCLEX exam and become a registered nurse is the educational credential for entry into addictions nursing practice. To meet the Healthy People 2020 objectives, all healthcare providers should be knowledgeable and competent to intervene across the continuum of substance use and the lifespan. Thus, the present gap in the education of nurses carries serious implications. The chance that a nurse will meet a person whose substance use puts him or her at risk for adverse health consequences is high. Focusing nursing education on treatment of substance use and addictive disorders alone results in nurses being unprepared to intervene with patients with risky substance use or those engaging in potentially addictive behaviors. While it is important that nurses recognize symptoms of a substance use disorder, they must also recognize patients at risk for adverse consequences, such as a single episode of risky alcohol use that could lead to serious adverse health outcomes such as motor vehicle crash, drowning, or alcohol poisoning.

The lack of a standard for foundational knowledge related to addictions in prelicensure curricula hampers the establishment of a basic knowledge base for nurses wishing to specialize in addictions. Nurses often lack the knowledge or competence to deliver evidence-based care in the prevention and early treatment of adverse health consequences associated with substance use or other potentially addictive processes, such as gambling. This gap is due to the minimal number of hours allotted to addictions in prelicensure or graduate educational programs (e.g., Campbell-Heider et al., 2009; Pillon, Ramos, Villar-Luis, & Rassool, 2004; Mollica, Hyman, & Mann, 2011).

The current paradigm in baccalaureate nursing programs perpetuates this lack of knowledge due to a narrow focus on treatment of substance use disorders. Thus, graduating nurses often lack the knowledge needed to understand the complexity of the relationship between health across the lifespan, substance use, and engagement in other potentially addictive behaviors. For nurses wishing to specialize in addictions nursing, this gap raises serious issues related to obtaining adequate education and clinical competence. The knowledge needed goes beyond the basics to require an in-depth understanding of substance use and addictions across the continuum of use and the lifespan. This learning includes knowledge of the biological, psychosocial, behavioral, and public health perspectives, as well as an understanding of the relationship between substance use and adverse health consequences. Nursing education has not kept pace with the trend to reframe substance use and adverse consequences in a broader model. This model, embraced by the global community, encompasses the full lifespan of use across the continuum of substance use or engagement in potentially addictive behaviors. Nurses seeking to specialize must find alternative methods to increase their knowledge and clinical competency in this specialty area.

GRADUATE-LEVEL PREPARED ADDICTIONS NURSES

Graduate-level education prepares nurses to focus on the complex needs of individuals, groups, and communities affected by substance use and addictive disorders. The graduate nursing education may lead to a Masters in Nursing Science (MSN), Masters in Science with a nursing focus (MS), or a doctoral degree (DNP or PhD). Addictions nurses also obtain advanced degrees in other areas, such as public health, business, and administration. These graduate nurses have important roles in addressing the needs of individuals, groups, communities, and populations. For example, public health nurses focus on enhancing the health of populations. The population-based approach of public health nurses is ideal for addressing the global impact of substance use disorders.

Additionally, graduate-level nurses who are prepared to work with special populations are also well positioned to specialize in addictions nursing. Nurses with graduate preparation for women's health and populations across the lifespan (e.g., prenatal, neonatal, pediatric, and older adults), diverse settings (e.g., acute care, emergency departments, primary care), and caring for vulnerable populations (e.g., HIV, trauma, corrections) are in key positions to care for individuals, families, and groups affected by alcohol and other drugs.

Graduate-level prepared nurses in roles as nurse educators have significant opportunities in education of the current and future nursing workforce. The major deficits in nursing education related to substance use and addictive disorders create a gap that can be closed by nurse educators from healthcare organizations to higher education. Graduate nurses in leadership positions from the unit to the organizational/system levels are instrumental in the design and implementation of prevention, intervention, treatment, and recovery programs for substance use and addictive disorders. These leaders are in key roles to promote the wide dissemination of evidence-based practices for individuals, groups, communities, and populations.

ADVANCED PRACTICE REGISTERED NURSES

The advanced practice registered nurse (APRN) who specializes in addictions holds a master's degree or higher and is in a role to address the needs of the population, or is in a direct care role consistent with *Consensus Model for APRN Regulation: Licensure, Accreditation, Certification, and Education* (APRN Joint Dialogue Group, 2008). These direct care advanced practice registered nurses who specialize in addictions include the certified registered nurse anesthetist (CRNA), certified nurse-midwife (CNM), clinical nurse specialist (CNS), and certified nurse practitioner (CNP).

Advanced practice registered nurses in these roles serve as leaders, consultants, change agents, and direct care providers—critical roles for reducing the harm related to use of alcohol, tobacco, and other drugs in the global society. Strobbe (2013) highlights the important role for nurse practitioners in addressing substance use among their primary care patients and identifies several clinical resources for nurses to help prevent, identify, and treat substance use at earlier stages across the lifespan. Finnell, Garbin, and Scarborough (2004) describe the APRN role and identify specific areas that differentiate the advanced practice registered nurse certified in addictions from the generalist addictions registered nurse (see Table 1).

Table 1. Areas of the Advanced Practice Registered Nurse Practice Beyond the Generalist Registered Nurse Role in Addictions (Finnell et al., 2004, p. 39)
■ Clients within the family system
■ Case finding/continuum of care
■ Theory integrated where appropriate
■ Groups/therapeutic role of nurse/group dynamics
■ Education of families and public about addictions
■ More emphasis on critical thinking, reasoning
■ Cultural needs of client and family
■ Teaching problem-solving to client and family
■ Primary prevention activities
■ Application of change theory
■ Psychobiology (e.g., neurotransmitters)
■ Monitoring client response to medications
■ Application of research to practice
■ Quality/performance improvement; outcome measures/benchmarking
■ Pain management
■ Legal/ethical issues

Advanced practice registered nurses who specialize in addictions build on their foundational graduate nursing education for their role through advanced knowledge and competence, gained through specialty continuing education and/or formal courses in higher education institutions. The APRN specializing in addictions needs to be knowledgeable and competent to address the needs of individuals, families, communities, and populations in the prevention, intervention, treatment, and management of addictive disorders. Advanced practice registered nurses also know when and how to collaborate with and seek consultation from other professionals and specialists in addictions.

DOCTORALLY PREPARED NURSES
Doctorally prepared nurses have key roles in addictions nursing. Several compelling reasons support increasing the proportion of research-focused and practice-focused doctorally prepared nurses. Research-focused nurses with the doctor of philosophy degree (PhD) or a doctor of nursing science degree (DNS, DSN, or DNSc) are needed to develop the science, steward the profession, educate the next generation of nurses, define the profession's uniqueness,

and maintain its professional integrity (AACN, 2006). These addictions nurses can be instrumental in advancing understanding of health behaviors, improving outcomes for patients and families, and promoting the health and well-being of communities, especially of the most vulnerable populations. As educators, doctorally prepared nurses are critically important in designing and implementing curricula for preparing the future and current nursing workforce to address the continuum of substance use and behaviors that may become maladaptive.

Practice-focused doctorally prepared nurses build upon their generalist foundation acquired through a baccalaureate or advanced generalist master's degree in nursing. These doctor of nursing practice (DNP) graduates are prepared for advanced practice roles and leadership in clinical settings. The changing healthcare landscape requires practitioners, nurse managers, and executives who are prepared to address the increasing complexity of patient care and systems of care across the healthcare continuum. Research-focused and practice-focused doctorally prepared nurses are essential as full partners, with physicians and other health professionals, in redesigning health care for individuals affected by addictions in the United States.

Additionally, doctorally prepared nurses specializing in addictions are critically needed in academe. Nurse educators have recognized the need to close the quality gap and enhance curricular content and clinical experiences related to substance use and addictive behaviors (Campbell-Heider et al., 2009; Mollica, Hyman, & Mann, 2011; Savage, Dyehouse, Marcus, & Lindell, 2011). With enhanced opportunities for registered nurses and advanced practice registered nurses, the potential exists for a greater number of nurses, across all specialties, populations, age groups, and settings, to have knowledge and competencies related to substance use and addictive behaviors, and thus address the Healthy People 2020 objectives related to substance use (U.S. DHHS, 2011).

Data from a role delineation study commissioned in 2011 by the International Nurses Society on Addictions (IntNSA) provide a current snapshot of registered nurses and advanced practice nurses in this specialty (Fabrey & Irwin, 2012). This study was conducted to describe the activities of specialty nurses (e.g., certified addictions registered nurses [CARNs] and certified addictions registered nurseadvanced practice nurses [CARN-APs]) in sufficient detail to provide a basis to inform future activities related to certification, including certification examinations. Two separate surveys were conducted with 158 valid RN respondents for the RN survey and 63 valid respondents for the advanced practice registered nurse survey. The majority of the RN group was female (91%) and white (89%).

The largest proportion of the sample reported the highest degree in nursing as bachelor's (41%), followed by associate degree (35%), master's (15%), diploma (8%), and doctorate (1%). Of the 158 RNs surveyed, 122 (77%) were CARNs or CARN-APs and 70% were members of IntNSA. The role delineation study found the majority of the APRN group to be female (84%) and white (93%). The largest proportion of the sample reported the highest degree in nursing as master's (73%), followed by the doctorate (20%). The remainder of respondents reported having a bachelor's degree. These respondents may have held a master's degree in a health-related area that was previously allowed for the CARN-AP certification. Of the APRNs surveyed, more than half (52%) held the CARN-AP certification and 19% held the CARN certification. The majority (86%) of respondents were members of IntNSA.

Practice Settings for Addictions Nurses

In the past, addictions nursing was practiced almost exclusively in specialized alcohol and drug treatment facilities, often during tertiary stages of illness. With increased appreciation for the diverse settings in which nurses now encounter substance use and addictive disorders, across the broad continuum of health and illness, nurses in associated practice areas are actively encouraged to consider specialty certification in addictions nursing. Some of these highly complementary settings include, but are not limited to, maternalchild health and neonatal care, pediatrics, primary care, family practice, geriatrics, emergency and urgent care, trauma, oncology, and pain management. In addition, continuously expanded knowledge regarding neurobiological and developmental aspects related to substance use and addictive disorders, along with increased efforts to screen for alcohol and other drug use and the provision of evidence-based brief interventions, underscores the need for a shift in perspective toward primary prevention. Thus, there is a growing need for addictions nurses to intervene at the population level, such as with public health departments or in policy roles.

Across the 158 RNs surveyed in the role delineation study by Fabrey and Irwin (2012), the vast majority (80%) worked in a specialty treatment center and hospital, with the remainder working in community agencies, private practice, school, or primary care settings. Registered nurse respondents were from 34 states in the United States and 2 other countries (Canada, Japan). Of the 63 APRNs, more than half (51%) worked in specialty treatment centers and hospitals. The shift to community and outpatient settings for the APRN role was evident in their primary work sites: community agencies (24%), private practice (16%), primary care (3%), and school settings (6%). Advanced practice registered nurse respondents were from 29 states in the United States and one other country (Canada).

Addictions Nursing Professional Society and Certification

The International Nurses Society on Addictions is a professional specialty organization for nurses. Members include clinicians, educators, managers, and researchers who practice in a wide variety of settings, including treatment centers, hospitals, schools, private practices, primary care, and other community agencies. IntNSA believes that all nurses, regardless of their specialty or practice setting, can play a role in the promotion of healthy lifestyles and the early identification of people at greater risk for developing problems associated with substance use and behaviors that can lead to substance use and addictive disorders.

Founded in 1975 as a provisional component of the National Council on Alcoholism, the organization was initially named the National Nurses Society on Alcoholism and later broadened in scope to the National Nurses Society on Addictions. In 1997, the organization merged with the Drug and Alcohol Nurses Association and the Consolidated Association of Nurses in Substance Abuse. The organization's name was changed to the International Nurses Society on Addictions, with a vision to be a global leader in addictions nursing.

IntNSA's conference in 2010, *Learning from Each Other: A Global Perspective of Addictions*, provided a springboard for strengthening and growing international networks. With a strong membership base in the United Kingdom, IntNSA served to catalyze a Global Addictions Nursing Summit in June 2011. An outcome was the launch of the Global Addictions Nursing Network (GANN) on Facebook. The GANN is a nonorganizationally aligned international global network for addictions nurses and those interested in addictions (http://www.facebook.com/GlobalAddictionNursingNetwork). The GANN joins individual nurses and groups (e.g., the Association of Nurses in Substance Abuse [ANSA]; Drug and Alcohol Practitioners' Association of Aoteroa New Zealand [DAPAANZ]; Drug and Alcohol Nurses of Australasia [DANA]) in a smaller global community forum for sharing information relevant to addictions nurses worldwide.

Through the Addictions Nursing Certification Board (ANCB), IntNSA has taken the lead in providing certification for the specialty. In December 1989, the first certification examination was administered, leading to the designation of the first certified addictions registered nurse (CARN). In 2000, the certification examination for advanced practice registered nurses was administered, leading to the CARN-Advanced Practice (CARN-AP) designation. The number of nurses holding the CARN certification has steadily increased over time to more than 700 in 2012. Although fewer than 50 APRNs held the CARN-AP certification in 2012, specific strategies to promote this certification (Finnell, Garbin, & Scarborough, 2004) have been successful. Particular mention of these certifications, overseen by the Addictions Nursing Certification Board, has been made in a publication by the Office of National Drug Control Policy, Substance Abuse and Mental Health Services Administration, and Health Services and Resources Administration, which highlighted the major role of nurses in integrating substance use services into primary care (http://www.cimh.org/LinkClick.aspx?fileticket=rM9trv WvVcQ%3D&tabid=795).

IntNSA has nearly 600 members, with the majority located in the United States. On average, 160 nurses attend IntNSA's annual education conference. The peer-reviewed quarterly international *Journal of Addictions Nursing* is the official journal of IntNSA. The *Journal of Addictions Nursing* publishes peer-reviewed articles on current research, practices, and innovations as they relate to the field of addictions.

Addictions Nursing Roles

Registered nurses responding to the 2011 role delineation study (Fabrey & Irwin, 2012) had worked as an RN for an average of 25 years, with 14 years in the addictions nursing specialty and 8.5 years in the current position. The majority (82%) worked full time and 75% functioned exclusively as an addictions nurse. Respondent RNs were asked to estimate the percentage of time spent in performing their various duties. The most time was spent in providing direct patient care, followed by administrative duties, consultation with other health team members, and community outreach. The greatest proportion of RNs (48%) reported direct roles as a clinical nurse, consultant, or other direct patient care roles, with an additional 13% in a case manager role. About 30% of RNs were in management/administrative roles. Few RNs were also in roles related to education (3%) or research (2%). A small percentage of RNs (4%) reported having prescriptive authority; these respondents were likely master's-prepared nurses who were not certified at the advanced addictions practice level.

Advanced practice registered nurse respondents reported that they had worked as a registered nurse for an average of 29 years and more than 9 years as an APRN. APRNs reported having worked more than 15 years in the addictions nursing specialty. On average, APRNs had worked 7 years in their current position. The majority (84%) worked full time, with 65% of their time dedicated to functioning exclusively as an addictions nurse. Similar to the RN respondents, APRNs spent the most time in direct patient care, followed by administrative duties, consultation with other health team members, and community outreach. The greatest proportion of APRNs (67%) reported direct roles as a clinical nurse, nurse practitioner, consultant, or other direct patient care roles, with 10% in case manager or consultant roles. A smaller proportion of APRNs, compared to RNs, were in management/administrative roles (15% versus 30%). A few advanced practice registered nurses were also in roles as educators (5%) or researchers (3%). Nearly half (49%) of the APRNs reported having prescriptive authority (Fabrey & Irwin, 2012).

Values and Principles Guiding Addictions Nursing Practice

Nurses specializing in addictions embrace the following values set forth by IntNSA:

> *Excellence*: Reinvigorating efforts to improve quality of care and quality of life for all persons affected by substance use and maladaptive behaviors.

> *Compassion*: Recognizing the importance of helping others through caring. Instilling hope in those who feel hopeless and empowering those who are powerless.

> *Diversity*: Affirming and accepting the uniqueness of each person, including his or her ideals, values, culture, and ethnicity.

> *Integrity*: Respecting the dignity and worth of every individual, grounded on the understanding that substance use and addictive disorders, like other chronic health problems, can be prevented and treated (http://www.intnsa.org/about /index.asp).

Nurses in this specialty also subscribe to a key principle: namely, that substance use and addictive disorders are complex but treatable diseases that affect brain function and behavior (U.S. DHHS, 2009a). Nurses are better equipped to engage in conversations with individuals and their families when they understand the neurobiological impact of alcohol and other drugs, as well as the impact of maladaptive behaviors that can lead to substance use and addictive disorders. Further, sharing that knowledge through health teaching and health promotion may be useful in reducing the stigma associated with substance use and addictive disorders (Finnell, 2000). Nurses in this specialty recognize that these are not disorders of self-control, and know that the neuronal mechanisms for these disorders have been solidly delineated with animal models and human neuroimaging studies.

As holistic providers, nurses in this specialty recognize the complex interactions among the bio-psycho-social-spiritual areas affected by substance use and maladaptive behaviors. Genetic epidemiological studies have broadened and deepened understanding of these disorders, yet there is likely a complex interplay between genes and environment (Urbanoski & Kelly, 2012). Addictions nurses have a working knowledge of the underlying psychological factors, such as motivation, self-efficacy, and emotional and cognitive regulation, that can hinder or facilitate behavioral change. These specialty nurses are also cognizant of the impacts that interpersonal relationships, patterns of behavior and habits, lifestyle choices, and other social factors have on the health and quality of life of individuals, families, and communities.

Addictions nurses recognize the benefits of mutual support groups and can convey the potential gains from participation to their patients, to nurses in other specialties, and to other healthcare team members. Mutual support groups, including 12-step programs, represent a readily available resource for individuals with substance use disorders. These programs have demonstrated considerable effectiveness in helping substance abusers achieve and maintain abstinence and improve their overall psychosocial functioning and recovery (Donovan & Floyd, 2008). For example, Alcoholics Anonymous (AA) participation has been associated with better alcohol use outcomes. Spirituality is of central importance within AA, which has described itself as a "spiritual program of action" (AA, 2001, p. 85). Kelly and colleagues (Kelly, Stout, Magill, Tonigan, & Pagano, 2011) suggested that spiritual practices and beliefs may help AA members to attribute different meaning to stressful events or life experiences and mobilize additional motivation and behavioral coping. More specifically, Strobbe et al. (Strobbe, Cranford, Wojnar, & Brower, in press) found that self-report of a spiritual awakening predicted improved drinking outcomes in a Polish treatment sample. Addressing an identified gap in the literature,

Strobbe and colleagues (Strobbe, Hagerty, & Boyd, 2012) also examined the phenomena of alcoholism and recovery in AA from a theoretical perspective, using the nursing Theory of Human Relatedness.

Ethics in Addictions Nursing Practice

Ethical concerns in addictions nursing practice are often complex and multi-dimensional, and may or may not be addressed in laws and professional ethics codes (Corey, Corey, & Callanan, 1998). Codes of ethical practice educate and inform professionals about sound ethical behavior, while mandating a minimal standard of practice. *Code of Ethics for Nurses with Interpretive Statements* (ANA, 2001) provides a framework for ethical nursing practice in addictions. Specific examples are provided for each of the nine provisions of the Code.

Provision 1: The nurse, in all professional relationships, practices with compassion and respect for the inherent dignity, worth, and uniqueness of every individual, unrestricted by considerations of social or economic status, personal attributes, or the nature of health problems.

Compassion is a key value of IntNSA and addictions nursing. Compassion means that addictions nurses recognize the importance of helping others through caring. Compassion entails the instillation of hope in those who feel hopeless and the empowerment of those who are powerless as a result of substance use disorders and other addictive behaviors. Respect is another key value of IntNSA. Addictions nurses respect the dignity and worth of every individual, based on the understanding that substance use and addictive disorders, like other chronic health problems, can be prevented and treated. Hence, addictions nurses are staunch patient advocates in helping to overcome negative attitudes and beliefs related to addictions to ensure appropriate, compassionate, and respectful care.

Provision 2: The nurse's primary commitment is to the patient, whether an individual, family, group, or community.

Addictions nurses recognize that substance use and maladaptive behaviors that can become addictive affect the individual, the family and other groups, and society as a whole. There is a progressive sequence of events, though the pace and intensity of consequences are different for individuals and family. Grounded on the understanding that these are brain-based disorders, addictions nurses appreciate the powerlessness that individuals experience in continuing to use (or behave) despite significant consequences, the securing of the substance or pursuit of the activity, or loss of control over use of the substance or activity. Addictions nurses also understand the behavior change process, and recognize that setbacks will occur during the progress toward the initiation or maintenance of a behavior change goal (e.g., abstinence from substance use).

Reversion to the target behavior, or *relapse*, is best conceptualized as a dynamic, ongoing process rather than a discrete or terminal event (Hendershot, Witkiewitz, George, & Marlatt, 2011). With this understanding, addictions nurses do not take a punitive stance toward those who return to the use of alcohol or other drugs, or who return to behavior that is maladaptive (i.e., relapse). Because they understand the pathophysiology of craving, tolerance, and withdrawal, addictions nurses are keen to identify individuals who may require medical detoxification or limited access to substance use or activities that may lead to maladaptive behavior to ensure a safe environment where associated harms are reduced. To support ongoing abstinence, addictions nurses actively work to promote relapse prevention skills among individuals affected by addictions, as well as their families and other groups.

Provision 3: The nurse promotes, advocates for, and strives to protect the health, safety, and rights of the patient.

Stemming from legislation in the early 1970s, confidentiality in the substance abuse field is governed by federal law (42 U.S.C. § 290dd-2) and regulations (42 C.F.R. pt. 2) (Office of the Federal Registrar, 2003). Thus, long before the Health Insurance Portability and Accountability Act of 1996 (HIPAA), addictions nurses were steeped in the practice of strict confidentiality of information about all persons receiving substance abuse prevention and treatment services. The law and regulations are more restrictive of communications than are those governing the doctorclient relationship or the attorney-client privilege. They are designed to protect privacy rights and thereby attract individuals into treatment.

Provision 4: The nurse is responsible and accountable for individual nursing practice and determines the appropriate delegation of tasks consistent with the nurse's obligation to provide optimum patient care.

Addictions professionals reflect a broad diversity. The specific proficiencies, skills, levels of involvement with clients, and scope of practice vary widely among specializations (e.g., physicians, nurses, social workers, psychologists, addictions counselors, peer counselors, sponsors). These roles often become blurred with inappropriate functions subsumed by healthcare providers working outside their scope of practice (e.g., assessment or diagnosis by a nonlicensed provider and/or noncertified provider), academic preparation, training, or competency. Competence comprises an expected and measureable level of nursing performance that integrates knowledge, skills, abilities, and judgment, based on established scientific knowledge and expectations for nursing practice. Addictions nurses often work in settings where nursing administration may not be dominant or even present. Thus, addictions nurses must be able to articulate their competence as well as their scope of practice; be aware of the professional standards that guide other team members (e.g., addictions counselors); and know the knowledge, skills, and abilities that all addictions providers have in common.

Personal behaviors and attitudes can conflict with ethical guidelines. Addictions nurses must be open to exploring and reconciling their personal experiences. They must also have a keen awareness of boundary issues with healthcare consumers, whether patients, their families, or the community and other groups. Addictions nurses are willing to participate in self, peer, and supervisory assessment of clinical skills and practice.

Provision 5: The nurse owes the same duties to others, including the responsibility to preserve integrity and safety, to maintain competence, and to continue personal growth.

Historically, addictions nurses and other addictions healthcare providers have not been positively viewed by their colleagues. The stigma associated with addictions in general may have tainted the perceptions of others in the healthcare field. However, with more widespread understanding and acceptance of addictions as brain-based disorders and other scientific advances in knowledge of addiction, accompanied by initiatives for population-based screening, interest in and support of careers in addictions nursing will increase. It is essential that addictions nurses accord moral worth and dignity to all human beings. This moral respect extends to oneself and to others, including nurse colleagues whose practice may be impaired as a result of substance use. Addictions nurses render respectful and skilled care, understanding that lifelong learning is critical for professional growth and competence. Addictions nurses are in key roles to change prevailing negative perceptions and attitudes toward individuals with substance use and maladaptive behaviors.

Provision 6: The nurse participates in establishing, maintaining, and improving healthcare environments and conditions of employment conducive to the provision of quality health care and consistent with the values of the profession through individual and collective action.

Given their knowledge, skills, and abilities, addictions nurses are often the first to recognize substance use or behaviors, such as gambling or Internet addiction in the workplace. Nurse leaders have been instrumental in establishing peer assistance services (e.g., Peer Assistance Services, Denver, Colorado) and model alternative-to-discipline programs (e.g., New York State Nurses Association [NYSNA] Statewide Peer Assistance for Nurses [SPAN] program). These programs are grounded in the recognition that problems faced by colleagues with drug or alcohol problems have an impact on patient safety and violate the public trust. Position statements, such as the NYSNA Fitness for Duty statement (http://www.nysna.org/practice/positions/fitness_for_duty.htm), focus on impaired practice rather than "impaired nurse." Such nuanced language focuses on the physiological and psychological fitness related directed to the ability to perform assigned duties rather than the morality of the person. Through model programs such as SPAN, voluntary surrender of license, and support for nurses in recovery to reenter the workforce, nurses demonstrate their humanity to their peers and support of the Americans with Disabilities Act to not discriminate based on alcohol or other drug abuse problems.

Provision 7: The nurse participates in the advancement of the profession through contributions to practice, education, administration, and knowledge development.

The research-to-practice gap is a major concern in prevention of addictions and in addictions treatment delivery. Addictions nurses have an ethical obligation to be knowledgeable of, and apply, evidence-based practice guidelines, inclusive of risk assessment and management. Addictions nurses need to engage in continuous quality improvement efforts to promote the highest quality of care for individuals, families, and populations affected by alcohol, tobacco, and other drugs of abuse, as well as maladaptive behaviors that can become addictive. The addictions nurse employs a wide range of contemporary best practices addressing the continuum of substance use and addictive behaviors.

Provision 8: The nurse collaborates with other health professionals and the public in promoting community, national, and international efforts to meet health needs.

Addictions nurses engage in partnerships with other specialty nurses (e.g., psychiatric mental health nursing, pain management nursing, emergency nursing), government agencies (e.g., SAMHSA), and the larger nursing community (e.g., Joining Forces) to promote the societal benefits of prevention, treatment, and recovery to affected individuals, groups, and populations. For example, by actively engaging in Recovery Month (September), addictions nurses help spread the message that addressing substance use and maladaptive behaviors is essential to overall health: that prevention works, treatment is effective, and people can and do recover.

Provision 9: The profession of nursing, as represented by associations and their members, is responsible for articulating nursing values, for maintaining the integrity of the profession and its practice, and for shaping social policy.

With a central role for advocacy, addictions nurses promote an environment in which the human rights, values, customs, and spiritual beliefs of the individual, family, and community are respected. Addictions nursing is continuing to evolve, yet a fundamental tenet is that health care is a human right for all. Preserving this trust is not the sole domain or responsibility of addictions nurses. Therefore, addictions nurses recognize the importance of direct human interactions, communication, and professional collaboration. These relationships may be with individuals, with populations, and with other healthcare professionals and health workers, both within and between nurses and public representatives. Addictions nurses must value expertise, power, and respect for all. Within the larger nursing community, addictions nurses inform positions, such as nonpunitive alcohol and drug treatment for pregnant and breastfeeding women and their exposed children (ANA, 2011), in recognition that substance use disorders are treatable, and that nursing service is delivered with respect for human needs and values and without prejudice to advocate for this vulnerable population.

Current Issues and Trends Affecting Addictions Nursing

HEALTHCARE REFORM

The Affordable Care Act (ACA) legislation has catalyzed healthcare transformation in the United States. Although state action toward creating health insurance exchanges varies across the nation, the ACA places a new priority on wellness and prevention, aligned with the quest for nurses to identify persons who are at risk for substance use and addictive disorders and intervene early in the process. The ACA includes preventive care, primary care, transitional care, and chronic long-term care. Services for substance use disorders are required benefits in basic plans for individual and small-group markets, requiring that such services be provided along with other covered medical and surgical benefits.

Of critical importance is the principle that insurers cannot deny coverage, charge higher premiums, or place annual and lifetime caps on insurance for people with preexisting conditions, including substance use and addictive disorders. This reform enhances health care across the continuum of substance use and addictive disorders—from prevention to community-based services that promote and support recovery—for the current U.S. population, with an estimated 32 million people being added to the rolls by 2014. This means that more Americans with substance use and addictive disorders who previously could not access care, including those with mental disorders, will have access to life-saving treatments. There are opportunities in the ACA for reimbursement for registered nurses and advanced practice registered nurses to provide care that prevents the progression of substance use and addictive disorders and promotes health outcomes for those further along the continuum.

HEALTHCARE DELIVERY SYSTEM IMPACTS

In 2011, The Joint Commission (a U.S.-based nonprofit healthcare accreditation organization) included performance metrics related to evidence-based substance use screening, brief intervention, and referral to treatment (SBIRT) for all hospitalized patients in its *Specifications Manual for National Hospital Inpatient Quality Measures* (http://www.jointcommission.org/specifications_manual_for_national_hospital_inpatient_quality_measures/). Although these Joint Commission metrics are optional at this time, prospective payment for SBIRT provision augments the clinical incentive for hospitals to adopt them. Because registered nurses constitute the largest group of healthcare providers in hospitals, they play a critical role in the successful implementation of SBIRT in hospital settings, and subsequently in hospitals' (1) adoption of the metrics for hospitals choosing to track and report them, (2) achievement of the metrics, and (3) implementation of SBIRT to contribute to positive patient outcomes. In addition to helping ensure the delivery of high-quality SBIRT, nurses can be instrumental in increasing (1) the rate of hospitalized patients screened for alcohol use, (2) the rate of eligible patients receiving brief interventions, (3) the proportion of patients accepting referral for treatment among those referred, and (4) the proportion of discharged patients contacted within 30 days for follow-up (Finnell, 2012).

REGULATORY ISSUES

The Drug Addiction Treatment Act of 2000 (DATA 2000) permits qualified physicians (http://buprenorphine.samhsa.gov/waiver_qualifications.html) to treat persons with opioid addiction with buprenorphine. Under DATA 2000, qualified physicians can obtain a waiver from the separate registration requirements of the Narcotic Addict Treatment Act to treat opioid addiction with Schedule III, IV, and V opioid medications or combinations of such medications that have been specifically approved by the Food and Drug Administration (FDA) for that indication (http://buprenorphine.samhsa.gov/titlexxxv.html). Buprenorphine has been shown to be a safe and effective form of pharmacotherapy for the treatment of opioid dependence (Orman & Keating, 2009), including detoxification and maintenance therapy. The serious and growing misuse of opioids has resulted in limited patient access to this medication. IntNSA has published a position paper, "The Prescribing of Buprenorphine by Advanced Practice Registered Nurses" (Strobbe & Hobbins, 2012), recommending that DATA 2000 be amended to allow qualified APRNs to prescribe this pharmacological treatment.

Although APRNs are not currently authorized to prescribe buprenorphine for the treatment of opioid addiction, nurses have a key role in partnership with the physicians who are qualified to prescribe this medication. A technical assistance publication, *Buprenorphine: A Guide for Nurses* (Center for Substance Abuse Treatment [CSAT], 2009), underscores the importance and value of nurses caring for patients receiving buprenorphine in conducting screening, assessment, treatment monitoring, counseling, and support services, and promoting relapse prevention skills (CSAT, 2009). Therefore, nurses can effectively provide high-quality care to the full extent of their license and within the federal regulations for buprenorphine treatment (Marcus, Savage, & Finnell, in press). Importantly, individuals receiving care from addictions nurses and other professionals in a buprenorphine clinic report high levels of satisfaction, attendance, and treatment adherence (Strobbe, Mathias, Gibbons, Humenay, & Brower, 2011).

THE NATION'S PRESCRIPTION DRUG ABUSE CRISIS

The United States Food and Drug Administration (FDA) Amendments Act of 2007 gave the FDA authority to require a Risk Evaluation and Mitigation Strategy (REMS) from manufacturers to ensure that the benefits of a drug or biological product outweigh its risks (Meyer, 2009). On April 19, 2011, the FDA announced the REMS program for manufacturers of long-acting and extended-release opioids (U.S. FDA, 2013). This announcement coincided with the Office of National Drug Control Policy's (ONDCP's) announcement of a Prescription Drug Abuse Prevention Plan to address the prescription drug abuse epidemic (http://www.whitehouse.gov/sites/default/files/ondcp/issues-content/prescription-drugs/rx_abuse_plan_0.pdf). An estimated 33 million Americans, age 12 and older, misused extended-release and long-acting opioids during 2007; this was an increase of 5 million Americans from 5 years earlier (U.S. FDA, 2013). Opioid medications have benefit when used properly and are a necessary component of pain management, but pose serious risks when used improperly. Never before has the FDA implemented REMS on such a wide range of established drug classifications. The REMS for opioids is intended to safeguard patients and communities. This policy will also affect APRNs who are prescribers, RNs who provide direct care to patients who require these medications, and patients who become dependent on/addicted to these medications.

To proactively address the needs of the patients it represents, the American Society for Pain Management Nursing (ASPMN) convened a coalition of APRNs and physician assistants from multiple organizations, including the International Nurses Society on Addictions and others (American Academy of Nurse Practitioners, American Academy of Physician Assistants, American Association of Nurse Anesthetists, Hospice and Palliative Nurses Association, Oncology Nursing Society) who had a vested interest in responding to the impact of the REMS on prescribers, nurses, and patients. Several important recommendations arose from this joint work:

- Specific measures ought to be adopted to ensure safe opioid use, to decrease the mortalities associated with inappropriate or nonmedical use of opioids. Nurses in this specialty need to be cognizant of the fact that the current REMS applies only to long-acting and extended-release opioids. Given this, there may be a shift of prescribing patterns, creating different problems in terms of access and abuse.

- Safety in prescribing is of utmost importance; all providers prescribing opioids should be knowledgeable in risk assessment, screening, and ongoing monitoring. Education should be coordinated with state regulatory authorities and professional organizations, and include programs for all allied health professionals. Mandating such education may be important to ensure effective and safe prescribing, monitoring, and evaluating of patient responses. Nurses specializing in substance use and addictive disorders will have a key role in patient education regarding REMS, including providing information on appropriate use, safe storage, disposal, and emergency treatment measures.

- Nurses in this specialty, along with colleagues in other nursing special-ties, need to educate the public on this major public health crisis, the appropriate use of opioids, and the risks associated with misuse and use that is not monitored by a healthcare provider.

- As the REMS program is monitored to determine its effectiveness, the FDA will use the data to reevaluate the program. Nurses in the specialty of substance use and addictive disorders need to stay abreast of any policy changes that may affect their patients' safe and effective access to opioids for pain management and remain vigilant to potential depen-dency, whether associated with misuse or physiological dependence.

In response to the increasing rates of opioid analgesic prescribing and the con-comitant increases in misuse, adverse events, and deaths, the Center for Substance Abuse Treatment/Substance Abuse and Mental Health Services Administration (CSAT/SAMHSA) sponsored a number of initiatives to increase and enhance prescriber knowledge of how to safely prescribe and manage opioids in their respective clinical practices. IntNSA received a three-year subcontract (AAAP005) for a grant from SAMHSA to the American Association of Addiction Psychiatry (AAAP; 1H79TI023439-01), titled *Cooperative Agreement for Prescriber's Clinical Support System for the Appropriate Use of Opioids in the Treatment of Pain and Opioid-Related Addiction (PCSS-Opioids)*. In addition to being represented on the steering committee, IntNSA members with expertise in this area are provid-ing educational webinars throughout the grant period. This project was a natural outgrowth of the IntNSA 2011 conference with the American Society for Pain Management Nursing, which is also a partner on the AAAP grant.

EVIDENCE-BASED SCIENCE

Advances in neuroscience have informed understanding of substance use and addic-tive disorders as brain-based disorders. In 2011, the American Society of Addiction Medicine (ASAM) defined *addition as* "a primary, chronic disease of brain reward, motivation, memory and related circuitry" (ASAM, 2011, p. 1). Healthcare providers often have negative attitudes toward patients with unhealthy alcohol use that affect their willingness to work with this population (Crothers & Dorrian, 2011). Shifting to a science-based perspective could help diminish the blame and shame that is the stigma associated with addictions and, it may be hoped, remove barriers to available life-saving treatments (Marcus, Savage, & Finnell, in press).

Addictions nurses are needed to disseminate this neurobiological evidence to individuals, groups, families, and populations. Specifically, specialty nurses need to incorporate this knowledge in education of persons affected, directly and indirectly, by substance use and related maladaptive behaviors. An important message is that neurons in the brain compensate for injury and disease, adjusting their activities in response to new situations or to changes in their environment; this capacity translates into the brain's ability to reorganize itself by forming new neural connections throughout life, known as *neuroplasticity*. This capacity should provide hope and inspiration for treatment and recovery.

Specialty nurses are also instrumental in conveying this knowledge to nurses and other healthcare providers to raise understanding that addictions can be prevented and treated, and that recovery is possible. That is, by integrating information about the neurobiological base of alcohol disorders in their conversations with these at-risk individuals, nurses can be instrumental in reducing the individual's doubts about treatment and shift their paradigm from one of self-blame to self-management by understanding the neurobiological bases for alcohol abuse/dependence and behavioral and pharmacological treatments (Finnell & Nowzari, 2013).

SCREENING, BRIEF INTERVENTION, AND REFERRAL TO TREATMENT

Evidence-based practices for the prevention and management of at-risk alcohol use have largely originated from studies involving primary care or emergency/trauma patients, with a primary focus on physician-led screening and brief interventions for alcohol. However, more attention is now increasingly being paid to the feasibility and efficacy of nurse-delivered alcohol SBIRT (or its individual components) in primary care settings (Aalto, Pekuri, & Seppä, 2005; Andréasson, Hjalmarsson, & Rehnman, 2000; Babor, Higgins-Biddle, Higgins, Gassman, & Gould, 2004; Lock et al., 2006), emergency care (Brooker, Peters, McCabe, & Short, 1999; Desy & Perhats, 2008; Desy, Howard, Perhats, & Li, 2010), and hospital settings (Broyles, Rosenberger, Hanusa, Kraemer, & Gordon, 2012; Fahy, Croton, & Voogt, 2011; Groves et al., 2011; Owens et al., 2011).

Emergency nurses are also in key roles and positions to recognize patients who could benefit from a more in-depth assessment of their drinking behavior, thereby helping to prevent future alcohol-related harm, injury recurrence, and associated economic and societal costs (Emergency Nurses Association,

2009). Thus, there are opportunities for nurses across all practice settings to provide screening, brief interventions, and referral to treatment for alcohol and tobacco—two of the most serious public health concerns. A pocket guide for alcohol screening and brief intervention, condensed from the NIAAA clinician's guide (NIAAA, 2007), is a portable reference for nurses to guide screening, assess for alcohol use disorders, and provide brief interventions (http://pubs.niaaa.nih.gov/publications/Practitioner/PocketGuide/pocket.pdf). Addictions nurses have the enhanced knowledge and competencies to engage in motivational counseling discussions with individuals across the continuum of substance use and addictive disorders so as to provide brief interventions directed at identifying and resolving problems, building and executing personal coping and risk-reduction strategies, and reducing other sequelae of hazardous, harmful, or debilitating health and interpersonal behaviors.

ADVANCES IN PHARMACOLOGICAL TREATMENT OF ADDICTIONS

Substantial advances have been made in pharmacological treatments for use of alcohol and other drugs, as well as behaviors that may lead to addictions. A review by Vocci and colleagues (Vocci, Acri, & Elkashef, 2005) highlights the progress that has been made in developing "first-generation" medications for treatment of opioid and cocaine dependence. NIDA is a major support for the discovery and testing of new medications to treat the symptoms and disease of drug abuse. For example, nicotine and cocaine vaccines have been developed to prevent those drugs from exerting their rewarding effects on the brain; these vaccines are undergoing testing in humans, and a methamphetamine vaccine is in earlier stages of development (Shen, Orson, & Kosten, 2012).

New depot formulations of medications are being studied in different patient populations to address irregular medication-taking, and enhance effects to last for weeks instead of hours. These formulations may be particularly useful for patients with serious mental illness, such as schizophrenia and with a co-occurring alcohol use disorder. For example, naltrexone is an opioid antagonist used in the management of alcohol dependence. Monitored administration of oral naltrexone to individuals with schizophrenia has shown significant reductions in alcohol consumption, alcohol craving, and psychopathology scores (Batki et al., 2010).

Nurses in this specialty have the knowledge and skills to address the needs of patients who are not taking medications as prescribed. A large, randomized, controlled trial conducted by Anton and colleagues (2006) illustrates the valuable role of nurses in providing clinical interventions to support effective pharmacotherapy. That trial compared the efficacy of medications approved for treatment of alcohol dependence (naltrexone and acamprosate) in conjunction with medical management and/or a combined behavioral intervention to placebo. The goal of the medical management intervention was to promote the patient's recovery from alcohol dependence. In delivering medical management, nurses and other healthcare professionals provided patients with strategies for taking their medications and staying in treatment, provided educational materials about alcohol dependence and pharmacotherapy, supported the patients' efforts to change drinking habits, and made direct recommendations for changing drinking behaviors.

The study conclusions were favorable for naltrexone with medical management; the group receiving the combined behavioral intervention only had poorer outcomes than those receiving medical management plus medication or placebo (Anton et al., 2006). Savage (2008) pointed out that two-thirds of the healthcare professionals who delivered the medical management intervention were nurses. The favorable findings for predominantly nurse-delivered medical management underscore the importance of a holistic approach to treatment and recovery. That is, nurses recognize that medications alone are not the answer, and that all aspects of the person—physical, psychological, social, cultural, and spiritual—must be considered in the individualized plan of care.

The science of pharmacogenomics heralds a new future for pharmacological treatments for substance use and addictive disorders. *Pharmacogenomics* is a science that examines the inherited variations in genes that dictate drug response and explores the ways these variations can be used to predict whether a patient will have a good response to a drug, a bad response to a drug, or no response at all (National Center for Biotechnology Information, 2004). A deeper understanding of how a person's genetics affect his or her response to a therapeutic medication opens the door for the next generation of pharmaceuticals. Addictions nurses will need to augment their current knowledge base with science related to particular gene variants that show better responses to particular medications. For example, gene variants have been associated with better response to bupropion for smoking cessation and naltrexone for alcohol use. The future is one in which a patient's genetic background will be a major factor in selecting the most appropriate and cost-effective therapeutic course of action.

ADVOCACY TO REDUCE THE STIGMA AND PROMOTE THE BENEFITS OF PREVENTION AND TREATMENT

IntNSA has a long-standing role in advocating for individuals, families, communities, and populations affected by substance use and addictive disorders.

Established in 2008, the second week in September is designated as Addictions Nurses Week. This event occurs during National Recovery Month, sponsored by the Substance Abuse and Mental Health Services Administration. Social prejudices, negative attitudes, and stereotyped perceptions are still common in society and among healthcare professionals. IntNSA is involved as a Planning Partner in National Recovery Month activities. A key role for addictions nurses is to increase awareness about recovery from these disorders, with and without co-occurring mental disorders. In this capacity, nurses in this specialty help to decrease the stigma and increase awareness of the discrimination that exists for this population.

Addictions nurses have a long history of advocacy for peer assistance for nurses with impaired practice. Recognizing that treatment works and recovery is possible, nurses in this specialty have promoted alternative-to-discipline programs (Monroe, Pearson, & Kenaga, 2008). These programs, rather than taking a punitive approach, underscore the mandate of the Code of Ethics for Nurses that "nurses in all roles should advocate for colleagues whose job performance may be impaired to ensure that they receive appropriate assistance, treatment, and access to fair institutional and legal processes" (ANA, 2001, p. 15).

The American Society for Pain Management Nursing and IntNSA joined together in a position paper related to pain management in patients with substance use disorders. Importantly, the paper builds from the premise that patients with substance use disorders and pain have the right to be treated with dignity, respect, and the same quality of pain assessment and management as all other patients (Oliver et al., 2012). This collaborative advocacy for some of the most stigmatized patients highlights the ethical imperative for pain management nurses and addictions nurses to provide high-quality care and ensure that nurses across all treatment settings understand and address the needs of patients with persistent pain and addiction.

Addictions Nursing Research and Scholarship

Nurse researchers and scholars have contributed to explicating the role of addictions nurses and initiatives to enhance their knowledge and competence. They have also advanced understanding of substance use and addictive disorders among population subgroups, and among individuals with co-occurring psychiatric and medical disorders. Research has informed the development and testing of interventions, including evaluation of treatment outcomes along the continuum of substance use as portrayed in Figure 1. This section provides examples of literature published over the eight-year period since the previous edition of the scope and standards of addictions nursing practice (ANA & IntNSA, 2004).

THE ROLE OF ADDICTIONS NURSES

The role of the addictions nurse has become increasingly complex and varied; the recent literature focuses both on *substance-specific* assessment screening, treatment monitoring, and addictions counseling, as well as *substance use* generally. In addition to direct patient care, the role of addictions nurses in shaping policy to increase access to care and improve the quality of services for persons with substance use disorders is emphasized (Fornili & Burda, 2010). There is also empirical evidence that there are distinct stages of role development for addictions nurses, with the early stages being pivotal to retention in addictions nursing. In a qualitative study of addictions nurse specialists in the UK, Clancy, Oyefeso, and Ghodse (2007) identified five sequential stages of role development, with each stage being characterized by key features of role acquisition: (1) lack of knowledge/skills related to addictions, (2) development of confidence and ability to set boundaries, (3) acknowledgment of credibility by staff and patients, (4) clinical competence and mentoring of others, and (5) mastery and consultancy. Because failure to navigate the early stages was associated with early departure from addictions nursing, these researchers encourage matching of professional development opportunities to stage-specific competencies. Clancy and colleagues (2007) also encourage addictions nursing experiences for nursing students, given that prior experience facilitated recruitment into addictions nursing.

ADDICTIONS IN POPULATION SUBGROUPS

Addictions nursing research has also advanced understanding of the prevalence and determinants of substance use and factors associated with recovery in population subgroups. An exemplar is Tonda Hughes's ongoing program of research related to determinants of hazardous drinking in sexual minority women. Compared to exclusively heterosexual women, she found that sexual minority women (defined as *mostly* heterosexual, bisexual, *mostly* lesbian, or exclusively lesbian) had higher rates of hazardous drinking and key risk factors for hazardous drinking, child sexual abuse, and sexual revictimization (Hughes, McCabe, Wilsnack, West, & Boyd, 2010). She also found that among sexual minority women, sexual revictimization was the strongest predictor of hazardous drinking among women who identified as *mostly* heterosexual and *mostly* lesbian. In a related study, she and her colleagues found that although sexual minority men and women had higher rates of substance use and substance dependence than their heterosexual counterparts, there was considerable variation in substance use outcomes across different dimensions of sexual orientation (identity, attraction, and behavior), particularly among women (McCabe, Hughes, Bostwick, West, & Boyd, 2009).

COMORBID SUBSTANCE USE

Other recent literature has focused on substance use and comorbid psychiatric or medical disorders. Comorbidity implies interactions between the illnesses that can worsen the course of both (http://www.drugabuse.gov/publications/infofacts/comorbidity-addiction-other-mental-disorders). A body of nursing research has been conducted related to comorbid pain and substance use. Compton and her colleagues have shown that persons with opiate addiction have a significantly heightened response to pain—hyperalgesia—which does not appear to change appreciably over time regardless of methadone or buprenorphine maintenance therapy (Alford, Compton, & Samet, 2006; Compton, Canamar, Hillhouse, & Ling, 2012). Importantly, they found that gabapentin, used for the treatment of neuropathic pain, reverses opioid-induced hyperalgesia (Compton, Kehoe, Sinha, Torrington, & Ling, 2010). So that clinicians can differentiate appropriate versus inappropriate opioid use, researchers developed an instrument designed to evaluate and track behaviors characteristic of addiction in chronic pain patients who are on opioid therapy (Wu et al., 2006).

INTERVENTION DEVELOPMENT, TESTING, AND OUTCOMES

Research has also informed the development and testing of interventions, including evaluation of treatment outcomes along the continuum of substance use. Research related to the role of nurses in prevention and management of at-risk alcohol use (see the section "Screening, Brief Intervention, and Referral to Treatment" on pgs. 33–34) is emerging in the United States. Broyles et al. (2012) are conducting a three-arm randomized controlled efficacy trial of nurse-led alcohol brief intervention for hospitalized patients to determine its impact on patients' overall alcohol consumption, binge drinking, and alcohol-related problems. This trial (ClinicalTrials.gov, 2013) is among the first in the United States, if not the first, to examine the impact of nurses in this role.

At the acute care end of the continuum, several investigators have focused on the use of technology to deliver interventions for persons with substance problems, such as engaging family and friends in online substance abuse counseling (Alemi, Haack, Harge, Dill, & Benson, 2005), use of a mobile short message service in substance abuse follow-up care (Bjerke, Kummervold,

Christiansen, & Hjortdahl, 2008), online substance abuse counseling (Haack, Burda-Cohee, Alemi, Harge, & Nemes, 2005), telehealth for treatment of substance abuse in rural adolescents (Miller, 2005), and Web-based treatment for alcohol problems among rural women (Finfgeld-Connett & Madsen, 2008). These interventions are important because they have a broad reach and can be used in population groups for whom other interventions may not be feasible. At the prevention end of the spectrum, interventions have focused on reducing alcohol and/or tobacco use in pregnant women, such as by motivational interviewing for alcohol (Osterman, 2011) or tobacco use (Karatay, Kublay, & Emiroğlu, 2010), using drink size to talk about drinking during pregnancy (Witbrodt et al., 2007), and nurse-led workshops to prevent fetal alcoholism spectrum disorder (Caley, Riemer, & Weinstein, 2010) and on substance use prevention in adolescents (Campbell-Heider, Tuttle, & Knapp, 2009; Lowe, Liang, Riggs, Henson, & Elder, 2012; Huang, Chien, Cheng, & Guo, 2012; Santisteban, Mena, & McCabe, 2011; see Cazzell & Snow, 2008, for a review). With few exceptions, most investigators examined the immediate or short-term effects of interventions, but not the longer-term effects.

Nurse researchers and scholars are increasingly contributing to the literature with narrative literature reviews, systematic reviews, and original research. There is a multitude of single studies, however, which leads to a somewhat fragmented knowledge base. More programs of research are needed to ensure a more comprehensive understanding of addictions nursing. Additional research is needed on the contributions of addictions nurses as key members of the healthcare team. Such research will be increasingly important within the context of a reformed healthcare system. The greater emphasis placed on prevention of substance use and addictive disorders provides the opportunity for expanded roles for addictions nurses. Innovative models are needed to promote widespread implementation and sustained integration of nurse-delivered interventions to promote positive quality and cost-effective care.

Addictions Nursing: Preparing for and Maintaining Competence

Until a comprehensive curricular change is implemented, an online curriculum for nurses has been developed to provide knowledge related to alcohol use (Murray & Savage, 2010). Although this curriculum has not yet been released by the National Institute on Alcohol Abuse and Alcoholism, it provides a template for similar curricula to address the full spectrum of substance use and addictive disorders. Content for the NIAAA curricula includes genetics, neurobiology, prevention, screening, risky use, withdrawal, treatment, health consequences, and legal/ethical issues. The NIAAA outline provides a curricular framework that can guide development of the required knowledge base for nurses working in the specialty of addictions nursing and can help nurses wishing to specialize in addictions nursing identify areas in which they personally need increased knowledge and clinical competence.

All nurses practicing in the specialty of addictions nursing are expected to be lifelong learners. Such continuous quality improvement requires nurses' active engagement in opportunities to increase their knowledge and clinical competence and keep current professionally. This may include enrollment in formal education courses relevant to the field of addictions nursing or participation in continuing education programs specifically related to addictions.

As nursing educators expand undergraduate and graduate-level curricula to include the requisite knowledge and skills for addressing the entire spectrum of substance use and maladaptive behaviors associated with addictive disorders, enhanced continuing education for practicing nurses will simultaneously be needed to ensure an adequately prepared current and future nursing workforce. Increasing the capacity of the nursing workforce to deliver alcohol, tobacco, and other drug interventions will require a multifaceted approach—system-wide, capacity building, and professional development—to ensure quality outcomes (Roche, Pidd, & Freeman, 2009). IntNSA has a long history of addressing these issues via several means:

- *Continuing education and professional development*: IntNSA's annual educational conference provides opportunities for both continuing education and networking. Theme-based conferences bring evidence-based knowledge to a diverse audience. Continuing education articles are featured in IntNSA's official journal and provided through IntNSA's annual conference and Web-based offerings.

- *Publications*: The *Journal of Addictions Nursing* is published quarterly and features an article for continuing education credit. Special editions provide the opportunity to disseminate current research, as well as articles pertinent to practice, current issues, and innovations. Selected topics have included women and co-occurring disorders; international focus; nurses, health, and tobacco use; and prescription medication abuse. Regular columns are provided to keep readers abreast of current clinical issues (Clinical Reviews), web sites (Web

Watch), legislative concerns (Policy Watch), and information about medications used to treat substance use and addictive disorders and mental disorders (Pharmacology Corner). IntNSA's *Core Curriculum of Addictions Nursing* (2007) serves as a reference book and study resource for nurses specializing in addictions. Position papers and briefer Fact Sheets, such as one related to prescribing of buprenorphine, are posted on the IntNSA web site for ease of access.

■ *Certification*: Specialty certification in addictions nursing is available from the Addictions Nursing Certification Board (ANCB) for the practicing addictions nurse and the advanced practice registered nurse. The certified addictions registered nurse (CARN) has met the certification board's requirements related to experience and education required for practice at the generalist level. The certified addictions registered nurse–advanced practice (CARN-AP) has met the certification board's requirements related to experience and education required for practice at the advanced practice level. The CARN and the CARN-AP care for individuals, families, communities, and/or populations across the lifespan. The overall aim of addictions nursing practice is to meet the World Health Organization's call to reduce the harm associated with alcohol and tobacco (Blas & Kurup, 2010), as well as the harm associated with the use of other psychoactive drugs or other potentially addictive disorders, such as gambling. The *CARN Study Guide*, updated in 2013, is available in electronic form from http://www.intnsa.org/store/index.asp.

Summary of the Scope of Addictions Nursing Practice

Nurses specializing in the field of addictions have contributed substantially to the prevention and treatment of substance use and addictive disorders. To continue to have a positive impact in reducing the burden of disease related to substance use and maladaptive behaviors, nurses in this specialty must continue to enhance and promote the quality of care for individuals, families, communities, and populations across the lifespan. Registered nurses and advanced practice registered nurses specializing in addictions are needed in all practice settings to reduce the harm across the continuum of substance use and addictive disorders. Nurses in this specialty must remain current with the growing body of nursing research and research from the general field related to prevention, intervention, treatment, and recovery.

Standards of Addictions Nursing Practice

Significance of the Standards

The Standards of Professional Nursing Practice are authoritative statements of the duties that all registered nurses, regardless of role, population, or specialty, are expected to perform competently. The standards published herein may serve as evidence of the standard of care, with the understanding that application of the standards depends on context. The standards are subject to change with the dynamics of the nursing profession, as new patterns of professional practice are developed and accepted by the nursing profession and the public. In addition, specific conditions and clinical circumstances may also affect the application of the standards at a given time (e.g., during a natural disaster). The standards are subject to formal, periodic review and revision.

The competencies that accompany each standard provide evidence for compliance with the corresponding standard. The list of competencies is not exhaustive. Whether a particular standard or competency applies depends upon the circumstances. For example, a nurse providing treatment to an unconscious, critically ill healthcare consumer who presented to the hospital by ambulance without family has a duty to collect comprehensive data pertinent to the healthcare consumer's health (Standard 1. Assessment). However, under the attendant circumstances, that nurse may not be expected to assess family dynamics and impact on the healthcare consumer's health and wellness (Assessment Competency). In the same circumstance, Standard 5B. Health Teaching and Health Promotion, may not apply at all.

The Standards of Practice coincide with the steps of the nursing process. The nursing process includes six singular yet integrated actions of assessment, diagnosis, identification of outcomes, planning, implementation, and evaluation. The bidirectional interactions between each component convey that the process is not linear (see Figure 2). That is, the nursing process is cyclical and dynamic. Each action (assessment, diagnosis, identification of outcomes, planning, implementation, and evaluation) encompasses significant actions taken by registered nurses and forms the foundation of the nurse's decision-making. The standards may be applied at the individual, family, community, and/or population level.

FIGURE 2. The Nursing Process and Standards
of Professional Nursing Practice
(ANA, 2010A, P. 3)

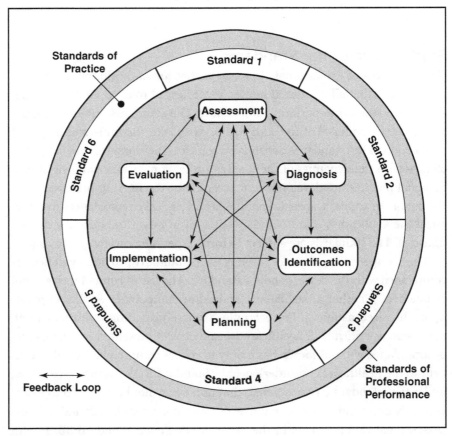

The public has a right to expect registered nurses specializing in substance use and addictive disorders to demonstrate competence (i.e., performing at an expected level) throughout their careers. The registered nurse is individually responsible and accountable for maintaining professional competence. The nursing profession is responsible for shaping and guiding any process for assuring nurse competence. Regulatory agencies define minimal standards of competence to protect the public. The employer is responsible and accountable to provide a practice environment conductive to competent practice. Assurance of competence is the shared responsibility of the profession, individual nurses, professional organizations, credentialing and certification entities, regulatory agencies, employers, and other key stakeholders (ANA, 2008).

Thus, competence in this nursing specialty must be evaluated by the individual nurse; nurse peers; nurses in the roles of supervisor, mentor, or preceptor; and by professional colleagues and patients. Through the Addictions Nursing Certification Board, IntNSA promotes two certifications (i.e., certified addictions registered nurse [CARN], certified addictions registered nurseadvanced practice [CARN-AP]). These certifications serve to maintain and promote quality nursing care by providing a mechanism for nurses to demonstrate their proficiency in this nursing specialty (http://intnsa.org/ANCB/index.asp). Although subjective and objective data about the nurse's knowledge base and actual performance can be obtained, no single evaluation tool or method can guarantee competence (ANA, 2008).

Standards of Practice for Addictions Nursing

Note: The healthcare consumer is defined to be inclusive of the individual, family, community, and/or population level.

Standard 1. Assessment

The addictions registered nurse collects comprehensive data pertinent to the healthcare consumer's health and/or the situation.

COMPETENCIES

The addictions registered nurse:

- Collects comprehensive data, including but not limited to physical, functional, psychosocial, emotional, cognitive, sexual, cultural, age-related, environmental, spiritual/transpersonal, and economic assessments, in a systematic and ongoing process while honoring the uniqueness of the healthcare consumer.

- Collects information on the amount, frequency, and pattern of alcohol consumption (based on the standard drink metric), drug use, tobacco use, and behaviors that may be maladaptive.

- Elicits the healthcare consumer's values, preferences, expressed needs, and knowledge of the healthcare situation, especially related to prevention and treatment of substance use and addictive disorders.

- Involves the healthcare consumer and other healthcare providers, as appropriate, in holistic data collection.

- Identifies barriers (e.g., psychosocial, literacy, financial, cultural) to effective communication and makes appropriate adaptations.

- Recognizes the impact of personal attitudes, values, and beliefs.

- Assesses family dynamics and impact on healthcare consumer health and wellness.

■ Prioritizes data collection based on the healthcare consumer's immediate condition, or the anticipated needs of the healthcare consumer or situation.

■ Uses appropriate evidence-based assessment techniques, instruments, and tools, such as the Alcohol Use Disorders Identification Test (AUDIT), Drug Abuse Screening Test (DAST), Alcohol, Smoking, Substance Involvement Screening Test (ASSIST), and a single screening question from Smith et al. (Smith, Schmidt, Allensworth-Davies, & Saitz, 2010; "How many times in the past year have you used an illegal drug or used a prescription medication for non-medical reasons?").

■ Synthesizes available data, information, and knowledge relevant to the situation to identify patterns and variances.

■ Applies ethical, legal, and privacy guidelines and policies to the collection, maintenance, use, and dissemination of data and information.

■ Recognizes healthcare consumers as the authority on their own health by honoring their care preferences.

■ Documents relevant data in a retrievable format.

ADDITIONAL COMPETENCIES FOR THE GRADUATE-LEVEL PREPARED SPECIALTY NURSE AND THE ADVANCED PRACTICE REGISTERED NURSE
The graduate-level prepared addictions nurse or the advanced practice registered nurse:

■ Initiates and interprets diagnostic tests and procedures relevant to the healthcare consumer's current status.

■ Assesses the effect of interactions among individuals, family, community, and social systems on health and illness.

Standard 2. Diagnosis

The addictions registered nurse analyzes the assessment data to determine the diagnoses or the issues.

COMPETENCIES

The addictions registered nurse:

- Derives the diagnoses or issues from assessment data.

- Validates the diagnoses or issues with the healthcare consumer, family, and other healthcare providers when possible and appropriate.

- Identifies actual or potential risks to the healthcare consumer's health and safety or barriers to health, which may include but are not limited to interpersonal, systematic, or environmental circumstances.

- Uses standardized classification systems and clinical decision support tools, when available, in identifying diagnoses.

- Documents diagnoses or issues in a manner that facilitates determination of the expected outcomes and plan.

ADDITIONAL COMPETENCIES FOR THE GRADUATE-LEVEL PREPARED SPECIALTY NURSE AND THE ADVANCED PRACTICE REGISTERED NURSE

The graduate-level prepared addictions nurse or the advanced practice registered nurse:

- Systematically compares and contrasts clinical findings with normal and abnormal variations and developmental events in formulating a differential diagnosis.

- Utilizes complex data and information obtained during interview, examination, and diagnostic processes in identifying diagnoses.

- Assists staff in developing and maintaining competence in the diagnostic process.

Standard 3. Outcomes Identification

The registered nurse specializing in addictions identifies expected outcomes for a plan individualized to the healthcare consumer or the situation.

COMPETENCIES

The addictions registered nurse:

- Involves the healthcare consumer, family, healthcare providers, and others in formulating expected outcomes when possible and appropriate.

- Derives culturally appropriate expected outcomes from the diagnoses.

- Considers associated risks, benefits, costs, current scientific evidence, expected trajectory of the condition, and clinical expertise when formulating expected outcomes.

- Defines expected outcomes in terms of the healthcare consumer, the healthcare consumer's culture, values, and ethical considerations.

- Considers the progression of substance use to disorder, the progression of behaviors that may become maladaptive and lead to addictive disorders, and the chronic and relapsing course of substance use and addictions.

- Includes a time estimate for the attainment of expected outcomes.

- Develops expected outcomes that facilitate continuity of care.

- Modifies expected outcomes according to changes in the status of the healthcare consumer or evaluation of the situation.

- Documents expected outcomes as measurable goals.

ADDITIONAL COMPETENCIES FOR THE GRADUATE-LEVEL PREPARED SPECIALTY NURSE AND THE ADVANCED PRACTICE REGISTERED NURSE

The graduate-level prepared addictions nurse or the advanced practice registered nurse:

- Identifies expected outcomes that incorporate scientific evidence and are achievable through implementation of evidence-based practices.

- Maintains practice grounded on evidence from neurobiology, such as the brain reward system, and how behavioral and pharmacological treatments and mutual support promote brain recovery following abstinence.

- Identifies expected outcomes that incorporate cost and clinical effectiveness, healthcare consumer satisfaction, and continuity and consistency among providers.

- Differentiates outcomes that require care process interventions from those that require system-level interventions.

Standard 4. Planning

The addictions registered nurse develops a plan that prescribes strategies and alternatives to attain expected outcomes.

COMPETENCIES

The addictions registered nurse:

- Develops an individualized plan in partnership with the healthcare consumer, family, and others considering the healthcare consumer's characteristics or situation, including, but not limited to, values, beliefs, spiritual and health practices, preferences, choices, developmental level, coping style, culture and environment, and available technology.

- Establishes the plan priorities with the healthcare consumer, family, and others as appropriate.

- Includes strategies in the plan to address each of the identified diagnoses or issues. These strategies may include, but are not limited to, strategies for:

  - Promotion and restoration of health;

  - Prevention of illness, injury, and disease;

  - The alleviation of suffering; and

  - Supportive care for those who are dying.

- Includes strategies for health and wholeness across the lifespan.

- Provides for continuity in the plan.

- Incorporates an implementation pathway or timeline in the plan.

- Considers the economic impact of the plan on the healthcare consumer, family, caregivers, and other affected parties.

- Integrates current scientific evidence, trends, and research.

- Utilizes the plan to provide direction to other members of the healthcare team.

- Explores practice settings and safe space and time for the nurse and the healthcare consumer to explore suggested, potential, and alternative options.

- Defines the plan to reflect current statutes, rules and regulations, and standards.

- Modifies the plan according to the ongoing assessment of the healthcare consumer's response and other outcome indicators.

- Documents the plan in a manner that uses standardized language or recognized terminology.

ADDITIONAL COMPETENCIES FOR THE GRADUATE-LEVEL PREPARED SPECIALTY NURSE AND THE ADVANCED PRACTICE REGISTERED NURSE

The graduate-level prepared addictions nurse or the advanced practice registered nurse:

- Identifies assessment strategies, diagnostic strategies, and therapeutic interventions that reflect current evidence, including data, research, literature, and expert clinical knowledge.

- Selects or designs strategies to meet the multifaceted needs of complex healthcare consumers.

- Utilizes established protocols to ensure standard safe care, such as the Clinical Institute Withdrawal Assessment (CIWA) and the Clinical Opiate Withdrawal Scale (COWS).

- Includes a synthesis of the healthcare consumer's values and beliefs regarding nursing and medical therapies in the plan.

- Leads the design and development of interprofessional processes to address the identified diagnosis or issue.

- Actively participates in the development and continuous improvement of systems that support the planning process.

Standard 5. Implementation

The addictions registered nurse implements the identified plan.

COMPETENCIES

The addictions registered nurse:

- Partners with the healthcare consumer, family, significant others, and caregivers as appropriate to implement the plan in a safe, realistic, and timely manner.

- Demonstrates caring behaviors toward healthcare consumers, significant others, and groups of people receiving care.

- Utilizes technology to measure, record, and retrieve healthcare consumer data, implement the nursing process, and enhance nursing practice.

- Utilizes evidence-based interventions and treatments specific to the diagnosis or problem.

- Provides holistic care that addresses the needs of diverse populations across the lifespan.

- Advocates for health care that is sensitive to the needs of healthcare consumers, with particular emphasis on the needs of diverse populations.

- Applies appropriate knowledge of major health problems and cultural diversity in implementing the plan of care.

- Applies available healthcare technologies to maximize access and optimize outcomes for healthcare consumers.

- Utilizes resources and systems within the healthcare setting and the community to implement the plan.

- Collaborates with healthcare providers from diverse backgrounds to implement and integrate the plan.

- Accommodates different styles of communication used by healthcare consumers, families, and healthcare providers.

- Integrates traditional and complementary healthcare practices as appropriate.

- Implements the plan in a timely manner in accordance with patient safety goals.

- Promotes the healthcare consumer's capacity for the optimal level of participation and problem-solving.

- Documents implementation and any modifications, including changes or omissions, of the identified plan.

ADDITIONAL COMPETENCIES FOR THE GRADUATE-LEVEL PREPARED SPECIALTY NURSE AND THE ADVANCED PRACTICE REGISTERED NURSE
The graduate-level prepared addictions nurse or the advanced practice registered nurse:

- Facilitates the utilization of systems, organizations, and community resources to implement the plan.

- Supports collaboration with nursing and other colleagues to implement the plan.

- Incorporates new knowledge and strategies to initiate change in nursing care practices if desired outcomes are not achieved.

- Assumes responsibility for the safe and efficient implementation of the plan.

- Uses advanced communication skills to promote relationships between nurses and healthcare consumers, to provide a context for open discussion of the healthcare consumer's experiences, and to improve healthcare consumer outcomes.

- Actively participates in the development and continuous improvement of systems that support implementation of the plan.

Standard 5A. Coordination of Care

The addictions registered nurse coordinates care delivery, programs, services, and other activities as needed to implement the identified plan.

COMPETENCIES

The addictions registered nurse:

- Organizes the components of the plan.

- Manages a healthcare consumer's care so as to maximize independence and quality of life.

- Assists the healthcare consumer to identify options for alternative care.

- Communicates with the healthcare consumer, family, and system during transitions in care.

- Advocates for the delivery of dignified and humane care by the interprofessional team.

- Documents the coordination of care.

ADDITIONAL COMPETENCIES FOR THE GRADUATE-LEVEL PREPARED SPECIALTY NURSE AND THE ADVANCED PRACTICE REGISTERED NURSE

The graduate-level prepared addictions nurse or the advanced practice registered nurse:

- Provides leadership in the coordination of interprofessional health care for integrated delivery of healthcare consumer care services.

- Synthesizes data and information to prescribe necessary system and community support measures, including modifications of surroundings.

Standard 5B. Health Teaching and Health Promotion

The addictions registered nurse employs strategies to promote health and a safe environment.

COMPETENCIES

The addictions registered nurse:

- Provides health teaching that addresses such topics as healthy lifestyles, risk-reducing behaviors, developmental needs, activities of daily living, and preventive self-care.

- Provides information about the definition of a standard drink, safe drinking limits, and risky alcohol use.

- Reinforces that no amount of alcohol or illicit drug is safe for women who are pregnant or intending to become pregnant.

- Advises on the risks associated with substance use and risk behaviors in general and for high-risk individuals in particular (e.g., adolescents, those with comorbid medical and mental disorders).

- Uses health promotion and health teaching methods appropriate to the situation and the healthcare consumer's values, beliefs, health practices, developmental level, learning needs, readiness and ability to learn, language preference, spirituality, culture, and socioeconomic status.

- Provides endorsed educational material related to substance use and other addictive disorders (e.g., Department of Veterans Affairs, National Institute on Alcohol Abuse and Alcoholism, National Institute on Drug Abuse, Substance Abuse and Mental Health Administration Services).

- Seeks opportunities for feedback and evaluation of the effectiveness of the strategies used.

- Uses information technologies to communicate health promotion and disease prevention information to the healthcare consumer in a variety of settings.

- Provides healthcare consumers with information about intended effects and potential adverse effects of proposed therapies, such as medications for alcohol dependence (e.g., naltrexone, acamprosate, disulfiram) and opioid addiction (e.g., buprenorphine).

ADDITIONAL COMPETENCIES FOR THE GRADUATE-LEVEL PREPARED SPECIALTY NURSE AND THE ADVANCED PRACTICE REGISTERED NURSE

The graduate-level prepared addictions nurse or the advanced practice registered nurse:

- Synthesizes empirical evidence on risk behaviors, learning theories, behavioral change theories, motivational theories, epidemiology, and other related theories and frameworks when designing health education information and programs.

- Conducts personalized health teaching and counseling considering comparative effectiveness research recommendations.

- Designs health information and healthcare consumer education appropriate to the healthcare consumer's developmental level, learning needs, readiness to learn, and cultural values and beliefs.

- Evaluates health information resources, such as the Internet, in the area of practice for accuracy, readability, and comprehensibility to help healthcare consumers access quality health information.

- Engages consumer alliances and advocacy groups, as appropriate, in health teaching and health promotion activities.

- Provides anticipatory guidance to individuals, families, groups, and communities to promote health and prevent or reduce the risk of health problems.

Standard 5C. Consultation

The graduate-level prepared addictions nurse or the advanced practice registered nurse provides consultation to influence the identified plan, enhance the abilities of others, and effect change.

COMPETENCIES FOR THE GRADUATE-LEVEL PREPARED SPECIALTY NURSE AND THE ADVANCED PRACTICE REGISTERED NURSE

The graduate-level prepared addictions nurse or the advanced practice registered nurse:

- Synthesizes clinical data, theoretical frameworks, and evidence when providing consultation.

- Facilitates the effectiveness of a consultation by involving the healthcare consumers and stakeholders in decision-making and negotiation of role responsibilities.

- Communicates consultation recommendations.

Standard 5D. Prescriptive Authority and Treatment

The advanced practice registered nurse uses prescriptive authority, procedures, referrals, treatments, and therapies in accordance with state and federal laws and regulations.

COMPETENCIES FOR THE ADVANCED PRACTICE REGISTERED NURSE
The advanced practice registered nurse:

- Prescribes evidence-based treatments, therapies, and procedures considering the healthcare consumer's comprehensive healthcare needs.

- Prescribes pharmacological agents according to a current knowledge of pharmacology and physiology.

- Prescribes specific pharmacological agents or treatments based on clinical indicators, the healthcare consumer's status and needs, and the results of diagnostic and laboratory tests.

- Evaluates therapeutic and potential adverse effects of pharmacological and nonpharmacological treatments.

- Provides healthcare consumers with information about intended effects and potential adverse effects of proposed prescriptive therapies.

- Provides information about costs and alternative treatments and procedures, as appropriate.

- Evaluates and incorporates complementary and alternative therapy into education and practice.

Standard 6. Evaluation

The addictions registered nurse evaluates progress toward attainment of outcomes.

COMPETENCIES

The addictions registered nurse:

- Conducts a systematic, ongoing, and criterion-based evaluation of the outcomes in relation to the structures and processes prescribed by the plan of care and the indicated timeline.

- Collaborates with the healthcare consumer and others involved in the care or situation in the evaluation process.

- Evaluates, in partnership with the healthcare consumer, the effectiveness of the planned strategies in relation to the healthcare consumer's responses and attainment of the expected outcomes.

- Uses ongoing assessment data to revise the diagnoses, the outcomes, the plan, and the implementation as needed.

- Disseminates the results to the healthcare consumer, family, and others involved, in accordance with federal and state regulations.

- Participates in assessing and assuring the responsible and appropriate use of interventions to minimize unwarranted or unwanted treatment and healthcare consumer suffering.

- Documents the results of the evaluation.

ADDITIONAL COMPETENCIES FOR THE GRADUATE-LEVEL PREPARED SPECIALTY NURSE AND THE ADVANCED PRACTICE REGISTERED NURSE

The graduate-level prepared addictions nurse or the advanced practice registered nurse:

- Evaluates the accuracy of the diagnosis and the effectiveness of the interventions and other variables in relation to the healthcare consumer's attainment of expected outcomes.

Addictions Nursing: Scope and Standards of Practice

- Synthesizes the results of the evaluation to determine the effect of the plan on healthcare consumers, families, groups, communities, and institutions.

- Adapts the plan of care for the trajectory of treatment according to the evaluation of response.

- Uses the results of the evaluation to make or recommend process or structural changes, including policy, procedure, or protocol revision, as appropriate.

Standards of Professional Performance for Addictions Nursing

Standard 7. Ethics

The addictions registered nurse practices ethically.

COMPETENCIES

The addictions registered nurse:

- Uses *Code of Ethics for Nurses with Interpretive Statements* (ANA, 2001) to guide practice.

- Delivers care in a manner that preserves and protects healthcare consumer autonomy, dignity, rights, values, and beliefs.

- Recognizes the centrality of the healthcare consumer and family as core members of any healthcare team.

- Upholds healthcare consumer confidentiality within legal and regulatory parameters, including the Health Insurance Portability and Accountability Act (HIPAA) and strict adherence to the Code of Federal Regulations (42 C.F.R. pt. 2).

- Assists healthcare consumers in self-determination and informed decision-making.

- Maintains a therapeutic and professional healthcare consumer–nurse relationship within appropriate professional role boundaries.

- Contributes to resolving ethical issues involving healthcare consumers, colleagues, community groups, systems, and other stakeholders.

- Takes appropriate action regarding instances of illegal, unethical, or inappropriate behavior that can endanger or jeopardize the best interests of the healthcare consumer or situation.

- Speaks up to question healthcare practice when necessary and appropriate for safety and quality improvement.

- Advocates for equitable healthcare consumer care.

**ADDITIONAL COMPETENCIES FOR THE GRADUATE-LEVEL PREPARED
SPECIALTY NURSE AND THE ADVANCED PRACTICE REGISTERED NURSE**

The graduate-level prepared addictions nurse or the advanced practice
registered nurse:

- Participates in interprofessional teams that address ethical risks,
  benefits, and outcomes.

- Provides information on the risks, benefits, and outcomes of
  healthcare regimens to allow informed decision-making by the
  healthcare consumer, including informed consent and informed
  refusal.

Standard 8. Education

The addictions registered nurse attains knowledge and competence that reflect current nursing practice.

COMPETENCIES

The addictions registered nurse:

- Participates in ongoing educational activities related to appropriate knowledge bases, professional issues, and the provision of safe, quality care to healthcare consumers (e.g., induction for buprenorphine).

- Demonstrates a commitment to lifelong learning through self-reflection and inquiry to address learning and personal growth needs.

- Seeks experiences that reflect current practice to maintain knowledge, skills, abilities, and judgment in clinical practice or role performance.

- Acquires knowledge and skills appropriate to the role, population, specialty, setting, role, or situation.

- Seeks formal and independent learning experiences to develop and maintain clinical and professional skills and knowledge.

- Identifies learning needs based on nursing knowledge, the various roles the nurse may assume, and the changing needs of the population.

- Participates in formal or informal consultations to address issues in nursing practice as an application of education and knowledge base.

- Promotes understanding of screening, brief intervention, and referral to treatment by sharing addictions-related knowledge with nurses in other specialties.

- Shares educational findings, experiences, and ideas with peers.

- Contributes to a work environment conducive to the education of healthcare professionals.

- Maintains professional records that provide evidence of competence and lifelong learning.

ADDITIONAL COMPETENCIES FOR THE GRADUATE-LEVEL PREPARED SPECIALTY NURSE AND THE ADVANCED PRACTICE REGISTERED NURSE

The graduate-level prepared addictions nurse or the advanced practice registered nurse:

- Uses current healthcare research findings and other evidence to expand clinical knowledge, skills, abilities, and judgment; to enhance role performance; and to increase knowledge of professional issues.

Standard 9. Evidence-Based Practice and Research

The addictions registered nurse integrates evidence and research findings into practice.

COMPETENCIES
The addictions registered nurse:

- Utilizes current evidence-based nursing knowledge, including research findings, to guide practice.

- Incorporates evidence when initiating changes in nursing practice.

- Participates, as appropriate to education level and position, in the formulation of evidence-based practice through research.

- Shares personal or third-party research findings with colleagues and peers.

ADDITIONAL COMPETENCIES FOR THE GRADUATE-LEVEL PREPARED SPECIALTY NURSE AND THE ADVANCED PRACTICE REGISTERED NURSE
The graduate-level prepared addictions nurse or the advanced practice registered nurse:

- Contributes to nursing knowledge by conducting or synthesizing research and other evidence that discovers, examines, and evaluates current practice, knowledge, theories, criteria, and creative approaches to improve healthcare outcomes.

- Promotes a climate of research and clinical inquiry.

- Disseminates research findings through activities such as presentations, publications, consultation, and journal clubs.

Standard 10. Quality of Practice

The addictions registered nurse contributes to quality nursing practice.

COMPETENCIES

The addictions registered nurse:

- Demonstrates quality by documenting the application of the nursing process in a responsible, accountable, and ethical manner.

- Uses creativity and innovation to enhance nursing care.

- Participates in quality improvement. Activities may include:

  - Identifying aspects of practice important for quality monitoring.

  - Using indicators to monitor quality, safety, and effectiveness of nursing practice.

  - Collecting data to monitor quality and effectiveness of nursing practice.

  - Analyzing quality data to identify opportunities for improving nursing practice.

  - Formulating recommendations to improve nursing practice or outcomes.

  - Implementing activities to enhance the quality of nursing practice.

  - Developing, implementing, and/or evaluating policies, procedures, and guidelines to improve the quality of practice.

  - Participating on and/or leading interprofessional teams to evaluate clinical care or health services.

  - Participating in and/or leading efforts to minimize costs and unnecessary duplication.

- Identifying problems that occur in day-to-day work routines in order to correct process inefficiencies.*

- Analyzing factors related to quality, safety, and effectiveness.

- Analyzing organizational systems for barriers to quality healthcare consumer outcomes.

- Implementing processes to remove or weaken barriers within organizational systems.

ADDITIONAL COMPETENCIES FOR THE GRADUATE-LEVEL PREPARED SPECIALTY NURSE AND THE ADVANCED PRACTICE REGISTERED NURSE
The graduate-level prepared addictions nurse or the advanced practice registered nurse:

- Provides leadership in the design and implementation of quality improvements.

- Designs innovations to effect change in practice and improve health outcomes.

- Evaluates the practice environment and quality of nursing care rendered in relation to existing evidence.

- Identifies opportunities for the generation and use of research and evidence.

- Obtains and maintains professional certification if it is available in the area of expertise.

- Uses the results of quality improvement to initiate changes in nursing practice and the healthcare delivery system.

---

* Board of Higher Education & Massachusetts Organization of Nurse Executives (BHE/MONE), 2006.

Standard 11. Communication

The addictions registered nurse communicates effectively in a variety of formats in all areas of practice.

COMPETENCIES

The addictions registered nurse:

- Assesses communication format preferences of healthcare consumers, families, and colleagues.*

- Assesses her or his own communication skills in encounters with healthcare consumers, families, and colleagues.*

- Seeks continuous improvement of her or his own communication and conflict resolution skills.*

- Conveys information to healthcare consumers, families, the interprofessional team, and others in communication formats that promote accuracy.

- Questions the rationale supporting care processes and decisions when they do not appear to be in the best interest of the healthcare consumer.*

- Discloses observations or concerns related to hazards and errors in care or the practice environment to the appropriate level.

- Maintains communication with other providers to minimize risks associated with transfers and transition in care delivery.

- Contributes her or his own professional perspective in discussions with the interprofessional team.

---

* BHE/MONE, 2006.

Standard 12. Leadership

The addictions registered nurse demonstrates leadership in the professional practice setting and the profession.

COMPETENCIES

The addictions registered nurse:

- Oversees the nursing care given by others while retaining accountability for the quality of care given to the healthcare consumer.

- Abides by the vision, the associated goals, and the plan to implement and measure progress of an individual healthcare consumer or progress within the context of the healthcare organization.

- Demonstrates a commitment to continuous, lifelong learning and education for self and others.

- Mentors colleagues for the advancement of nursing practice, the profession, and quality health care.

- Treats colleagues with respect, trust, and dignity.*

- Develops communication and conflict resolution skills.

- Participates in professional organizations.

- Communicates effectively with the healthcare consumer and colleagues.

- Seeks ways to advance nursing autonomy and accountability.*

- Participates in efforts to influence healthcare policy involving healthcare consumers and the profession.

ADDITIONAL COMPETENCIES FOR THE GRADUATE-LEVEL PREPARED SPECIALTY NURSE AND THE ADVANCED PRACTICE REGISTERED NURSE

The graduate-level prepared addictions nurse or the advanced practice registered nurse:

- Influences decision-making bodies to improve the professional practice environment and healthcare consumer outcomes.

---

* BHE/MONE, 2006.

- Provides direction to enhance the effectiveness of the interprofessional team.

- Promotes advanced practice nursing and role development by interpreting its role for healthcare consumers, families, and others.

- Models expert practice to interprofessional team members and healthcare consumers.

- Mentors colleagues in the acquisition of clinical knowledge, skills, abilities, and judgment.

Standard 13. Collaboration

The addictions registered nurse collaborates with the healthcare consumer, family, and others in the conduct of nursing practice.

COMPETENCIES
The addictions registered nurse:

- Partners with others to effect change and produce positive outcomes through the sharing of knowledge of the healthcare consumer and/or situation.

- Communicates with the healthcare consumer, the family, and healthcare providers regarding healthcare consumer care and the nurse's role in the provision of that care.

- Promotes conflict management and engagement.

- Participates in building consensus or resolving conflict in the context of healthcare consumer care.

- Applies group process and negotiation techniques with healthcare consumers and colleagues.

- Adheres to standards and applicable codes of conduct that govern behavior among peers and colleagues to create a work environment that promotes cooperation, respect, and trust.

- Cooperates in creating a documented plan, focused on outcomes and decisions related to care and delivery of services, that indicates communication with healthcare consumers, families, and others.

- Engages in teamwork and team-building processes.

ADDITIONAL COMPETENCIES FOR THE GRADUATE-LEVEL PREPARED SPECIALTY NURSE AND THE ADVANCED PRACTICE REGISTERED NURSE
The graduate-level prepared addictions nurse or the advanced practice registered nurse:

- Partners with other disciplines to enhance healthcare consumer outcomes through interprofessional activities, such as education, consultation, management, technological development, or research opportunities.

- Invites the contribution of the healthcare consumer, family, and team members in order to achieve optimal outcomes.

- Leads in establishing, improving, and sustaining collaborative relationships to achieve safe, quality healthcare consumer care.

- Documents plan-of-care communications, rationales for plan-of-care changes, and collaborative discussions to improve healthcare consumer outcomes.

Standard 14. Professional Practice Evaluation

The addictions registered nurse evaluates her or his own nursing practice in relation to professional practice standards and guidelines, relevant statutes, rules, and regulations.

COMPETENCIES

The addictions registered nurse:

- Provides age-appropriate and developmentally appropriate care in a culturally and ethnically sensitive manner.

- Engages in self-evaluation of practice on a regular basis, identifying areas of strength as well as areas in which professional growth would be beneficial.

- Obtains informal feedback regarding her or his own practice from healthcare consumers, peers, professional colleagues, and others.

- Participates in peer review as appropriate.

- Takes action to achieve goals identified during the evaluation process.

- Provides the evidence for practice decisions and actions as part of the informal and formal evaluation processes.

- Interacts with peers and colleagues to enhance her or his own professional nursing practice or role performance.

- Provides peers with formal or informal constructive feedback regarding their practice or role performance.

ADDITIONAL COMPETENCIES FOR THE GRADUATE-LEVEL PREPARED SPECIALTY NURSE AND THE ADVANCED PRACTICE REGISTERED NURSE

The graduate-level prepared addictions nurse or the advanced practice registered nurse:

- Engages in a formal process seeking feedback regarding her or his practice from healthcare consumers, peers, professional colleagues, and others.

Standard 15. Resource Utilization

The addictions registered nurse utilizes appropriate resources to plan and provide nursing services that are safe, effective, and financially responsible.

COMPETENCIES

The addictions registered nurse:

- Assesses individual healthcare consumer care needs and resources available to achieve desired outcomes.

- Identifies healthcare consumer care needs, potential for harm, complexity of the task, and desired outcome when considering resource allocation.

- Delegates elements of care to appropriate healthcare workers in accordance with any applicable legal or policy parameters or principles.

- Identifies the evidence when evaluating resources.

- Advocates for resources, including technology, that enhance nursing practice.

- Modifies practice when necessary to promote positive interaction between healthcare consumers, care providers, and technology.

- Assists the healthcare consumer and family in identifying and securing appropriate services to address needs across the healthcare continuum.

- Assists the healthcare consumer and family in factoring costs, risks, and benefits into decisions about treatment and care.

ADDITIONAL COMPETENCIES FOR THE GRADUATE-LEVEL PREPARED SPECIALTY NURSE AND THE ADVANCED PRACTICE REGISTERED NURSE

The graduate-level prepared addictions nurse or the advanced practice registered nurse:

- Utilizes organizational and community resources to formulate interprofessional plans of care.

■ Formulates innovative solutions for healthcare consumer care problems that utilize resources effectively and maintain quality.

■ Designs evaluation strategies that demonstrate cost-effectiveness, cost benefit, and efficiency factors associated with addictions nursing practice.

Standard 16. Environmental Health

The addictions registered nurse practices in an environmentally safe and healthy manner.

COMPETENCIES

The addictions registered nurse:

- Attains knowledge of environmental health concepts, such as implementation of environmental health strategies.

- Promotes a practice environment that reduces environmental health risks for workers and healthcare consumers.

- Assesses the practice environment for factors such as sound, odor, noise, and light that threaten health.

- Advocates for the judicious and appropriate use of products in health care.

- Communicates environmental health risks and exposure reduction strategies to healthcare consumers, families, colleagues, and communities.

- Utilizes scientific evidence to determine if a product or treatment is an environmental threat.

- Participates in strategies to promote healthy communities.

ADDITIONAL COMPETENCIES FOR THE GRADUATE-LEVEL PREPARED SPECIALTY NURSE AND THE ADVANCED PRACTICE REGISTERED NURSE

The graduate-level prepared addictions nurse or the advanced practice registered nurse:

- Creates partnerships that promote sustainable environmental health policies and conditions.

- Analyzes the impact of social, political, and economic influences on the environment and human health exposures.

- Critically evaluates the manner in which environmental health issues are presented by the popular media.

- Advocates for implementation of environmental principles in addictions nursing practice.

- Supports nurses in advocating for and implementing environmental principles in addictions nursing practice.

References and Bibliography

Aalto, M., Pekuri, P., & Seppä, K. (2005). Primary health care professional activity in intervening in patients' alcohol drinking drug: A 3-year brief intervention implementation project. *Drug & Alcohol Dependence, 69*(1), 9–14.

Adams, S., Leukefeld, C. G., & Peden, A. R. (2008). Substance abuse treatment for women offenders: A research review. *Journal of Addictions Nursing, 19*(2), 61–75. doi:10.1080/10884600802111648

Alcoholics Anonymous (AA). (1939). *Alcoholics Anonymous: The story of how thousands of men and women have recovered from alcoholism* (3rd ed.). New York: Alcoholics Anonymous World Services.

Alcoholics Anonymous (AA). (2001). *Alcoholics Anonymous: The story of how thousands of men and women have recovered from alcoholism* (4th ed.). New York: Alcoholics Anonymous World Services.

Alemi, F., Haack, M. R., Harge, A., Dill, R., & Benson, L. (2005). Engaging client's family and friends in online counseling. *Journal of Addictions Nursing, 16*(1–2), 47–55. doi:10.1080/10884600590917192

Alford, D. P., Compton, P., & Samet, J. H. (2006). Acute pain management for patients receiving maintenance methadone or buprenorphine therapy. *Annals of Internal Medicine, 144*(2), 127–134.

American Association of Colleges of Nursing (AACN). (2006). *The essentials of doctoral education for advanced nursing practice*. Washington, DC: Author.

American College of Surgeons Committee on Trauma (ACoSCo). (2006). *Resources for optimal care of the injured patient*. Chicago: ACoSCo.

American Nurses Association (ANA). (2001). *Code of Ethics for Nurses with interpretive statements*. Washington, DC: Nursesbooks.org.

American Nurses Association (ANA). (2008). *Professional role competence* (position statement). Silver Spring, MD: Author.

American Nurses Association (ANA). (2010a). *Nursing: Scope and Standards of Practice*, (2nd edition), Silver Spring, MD: Nursesbooks.org.

American Nurses Association (ANA). (2010b). *Nursing's social policy statement: The essence of the profession.* Silver Spring, MD: Nursesbooks.org.

American Nurses Association & International Nurses Society on Addictions. (2004). *Scope and standards of addictions nursing practice.* Washington, DC: Nursesbooks.org.

American Nurses Association, National Nurses Society on Addictions, & Drug and Alcohol Nurses Association. (1987). *Care of clients with addictions: Dimensions of nursing practice.* Kansas City, MO: American Nurses Association.

American Psychiatric Association. (2013). *Diagnostic and statistical manual of mental disorders* (rev. 5th ed.). Washington, DC: Author.

American Society of Addiction Medicine (ASAM). (2011). Public policy statement: Definition of addiction. Chevy Chase, MD: Author.

Anderson, P., Aromaa, S., Rosenbloom, D., & Enos, G. (2008). *Screening and brief intervention: Making a public health difference.* Join Together. Retrieved from http://www.jointogether.org/aboutus/ourpublications/pdf/sbi-report.pdf

Andréasson, S., Hjalmarsson, K., & Rehnman, C. (2000). Implementation and dissemination of methods for prevention of alcohol problems in primary health care: A feasibility study. *Alcohol & Alcoholism, 35*(5), 525–530.

Antai-Otong, D. (2006). Women and alcoholism: Gender-related medical complications: Treatment considerations. *Journal of Addictions Nursing, 17*(1), 33–45. doi:10.1080/10884600500505828

Anton, R. F., O'Malley, S. S., Ciraulo, D. A., Cisler, R. A., Couper, D., Donovan, D. M., et al. (2006). Combined psychotherapies and behavioral interventions for alcohol dependence: The COMBINE Study, a randomized controlled trial. *Journal of the American Medical Association, 295*(17), 2003–2017.

Apodaca, T. R., Miller, W. R., Schermer, C. R., & Amrhein, P. C. (2007). A pilot study of bibliotherapy to reduce alcohol problems among patients in a hospital trauma center. *Journal of Addictions Nursing, 18*(4), 167–173. doi:10.1080/10884600701698745

APRN Joint Dialogue Group. (2008). *Consensus model for APRN regulation: Licensure, accreditation, certification and education.* Retrieved from http://www.nursingworld.org/ConsensusModelforAPRN

Armstrong, M. (2008). Foundations for a gender-based treatment model for women in recovery from chemical dependency. *Journal of Addictions Nursing, 19*(2), 77–82. doi:10.1080/10884600802111663

Armstrong, M., & Holmes, E. (2005). Frequency of nurse practitioner screening for substance use disorders. *Journal of Addictions Nursing, 16*(3), 125–129. doi:10.1080/10884600500196644

Armstrong, M., & Miller, K. L. (2001). Concepts and meanings of cigarette smoking among children aged 10–16 years. *Journal of Addictions Nursing, 13*(3–4), 127–136. doi:10.3109/10884600109052647

Atkinson, J. S., & Whitsett, D. (2003). Severity of common personal and substance abuse related problems in low-income women: Implications for treatment. *Journal of Addictions Nursing, 14*(1), 27–33. doi:10.1080/10884600305369

Babcock, M. (2008). Substance-using mothers: Bias in culture and research. *Journal of Addictions Nursing, 19*(2), 87–91. doi:10.1080/10884600802111671

Babor, T. F., & Higgins-Biddle, J. C. (2001). *Brief intervention for hazardous and harmful drinking in primary care: A manual for use in primary care.* Geneva, Switzerland: World Health Organization.

Babor, T. F., Higgins-Biddle, J. C., Higgins, P., Gassman, R. A., & Gould, B. E. (2004). Training medical providers to conduct alcohol screening and brief interventions. *Substance Abuse, 25*(1), 17–26.

Bager, P., & Vilstrup, H. (2010). Post-discharge brief intervention increases the frequency of alcohol abstinence—A randomized trial. *Journal of Addictions Nursing, 21*(1), 37–41. doi:10.3109/10884601003628104

Baldacchino, A., & Rassool, G. H. (2006). The self-help movement in the addiction field—Revisited. *Journal of Addictions Nursing, 17*(1), 47–52. doi:10.1080/10884600500505836

Batki, S. L., Dimmock, J. A., Wade, M., Gately, P. W., Cornell, M., Maisto, S. A., Carey, K. B., & Ploutz-Snyder, R. (2010). Monitored naltrexone without counseling for alcohol abuse/dependence in schizophrenia-spectrum disorders. *American Journal on Addictions, 16*(4), 253–259.

Belcher, J. R., Greene, J. A., McAlpine, C., & Ball, K. (2001). Considering pathways into homelessness: Mothers, addictions, and trauma. *Journal of Addictions Nursing, 13*(3–4), 199–208. doi:10.3109/10884600109052654

Beyer, S. (2004). Cardiovascular disease in alcohol abusers. *Journal of Addictions Nursing, 15*(2), 75–79. doi:10.1080/10884600490450209

Bjerke, T. N., Kummervold, P. E., Christiansen, E. K., & Hjortdahl, P. (2008). "It made me feel connected"—An exploratory study on the use of mobile SMS in follow-up care for substance abusers. *Journal of Addictions Nursing, 19*(4), 195–200. doi:10.1080/10884600802504735

Blas, E., & Kurup, A. S. (Eds.). (2010). *World Health Organization: Equity, social determinants and public health programs.* Retrieved from http://whqlibdoc.who.int/publications/2010/9789241563970_eng.pdf

Board of Higher Education & Massachusetts Organization of Nurse Executives (BHE/MONE). (2006). *Creativity and connections: Building the framework for the future of nursing education.* Report from the Invitational Working Session, March 23–24, 2006. Burlington, MA: MONE. Available at http://www.mass.edu/currentinit/documents/NursingCreativityAndConnections.pdf

Bogart, C. J., & Pearce, C. E. (2003). "13th-stepping": Why Alcoholics Anonymous is not always a safe place for women. *Journal of Addictions Nursing, 14*(1), 43–47. doi:10.1080/10884600305373

Boyd, C. J., McCabe, S. E., & d'Arcy, H. (2004). Collegiate living environments: A predictor of binge drinking, negative consequences, and risk-reducing behaviors. *Journal of Addictions Nursing, 15*(3), 111–118. doi:10.1080/10884600490491204

Boyle, A. R., & Davis, H. (2006). Early screening and assessment of alcohol and substance abuse in the elderly: Clinical implications. *Journal of Addictions Nursing, 17*(2), 95–103. doi:10.1080/10884600600668229

Brooker, C., Peters, J., McCabe, C., & Short, N. (1999). The views of nurses to the conduct of a randomised controlled trial of problem drinkers in an accident and emergency department. *International Journal of Nursing Studies, 36*(1), 33–39.

Brown, E. J. (2006). Good mother, bad mother: Perception of mothering by rural African-American women who use cocaine. *Journal of Addictions Nursing, 17*(1), 21–31. doi:10.1080/10884600500505802

Brown, N. K. (2001). Women and crack-cocaine: Identifying high-risk behavior in recovery. *Journal of Addictions Nursing, 13*(3–4), 187–197. doi:10.3109/10884600109052653

Brown, N. K. (2003). Relapsing, running, and relieving: A model for high-risk behavior in recovery. *Journal of Addictions Nursing, 14*(1), 11–17. doi:10.1080/10884600305372

Broyles, L., Rosenberger, E., Hanusa, B., Kraemer, K., & Gordon, A. (2012). Hospitalized patients' acceptability of nurse-delivered screening, brief intervention, and referral to treatment (SBIRT). *Alcoholism: Clinical & Experimental Research, 36*(4), 725–731.

Caley, L. M., Riemer, S., & Weinstein, H. S. (2010). Results of a nurse-led workshop designed to prevent Fetal Alcohol Spectrum Disorder. *Public Health Nursing, 27*(3), 232–239.

Campbell-Heider, N. C., Finnell, D. S., Feigenbaum, J. C., et al. (2009). Survey on addictions: Towards curricular change for family nurse practioners. *International Journal of Nursing Education Scholarship, 6*, 1–17.

Campbell-Heider, N. C., Tuttle, J., Bidwell-Cerone, S., Richeson, G. T., & Collins, S. E. (2003). The buffering effects of connectedness: Teen Club intervention for children of substance abusing families. *Journal of Addictions Nursing, 14*(4), 175–182. doi:10.1080/jan.14.4.175.182

Campbell-Heider, N. C., Tuttle, J., & Knapp, T. R. (2009). CE FEATURE: The effect of positive adolescent life skills training on long-term outcomes for high-risk teens. *Journal of Addictions Nursing, 20*(1), 6–15. doi:10.1080/10884600802693165

Cazzell, M., & Snow, D. (2008). Adolescent intervention research. *Journal of Addictions Nursing, 19*(3), 165–169. doi:10.1080/10884600802306065

Center for Substance Abuse Treatment. (2009). *Buprenorphine: A guide for nurses* (DHHS Publication No. (SMA) 09-4376). Rockville, MD: Substance Abuse and Mental Health Services Administration.

Chang, Y-P., Wray, L. O., Sessanna, L., & Peng, H.-L. (2011). Use of prescription opioid medication among community-dwelling older adults with noncancer chronic pain. *Journal of Addictions Nursing, 22* (1–2), 19–24. doi:10.3109/10884602.2010.545088

Cherpitel, C. J., Bernstein, E., Bernstein, J., Moskalewicz, J., & Swiatkiewicz, G. (2009). Screening, brief intervention and referral to treatment (SBIRT) in a Polish emergency room: Challenges in cultural translation of SBIRT. *Journal of Addictions Nursing, 20*(3), 127–131. doi:10.1080/10884600903047618

Clancy, C., Oyefeso, A., & Ghodse, H. (2007). Role development and career stages in addiction nursing: An exploratory study. *Journal of Advanced Nursing, 57*(2), 161–171.

ClinicalTrials.gov. (2013). Behavior change for hospitalized veterans ("A service of the National Institutes of Health.") April. Retrieved from http://www.clinicaltrials.gov/ct2/show/NCT01602172?term=Health+Behavior+Change+for+Hospitalized+Veterans&rank=1

Committee on Health Care for Underserved Women, American College of Obstetrics and Gynecologists. (2011). At-risk drinking and alcohol dependence: Obstetric and gynecologic implications. *Obstetrics & Gynecology, 118*(2), 383–388.

Compton, P. (2011). Treating chronic pain with prescription opioids in the substance abuser: Relapse prevention and management. *Journal of Addictions Nursing, 22*(1–2), 39–45. doi:10.3109/10884602.2010.545092

Compton, P., Canamar, C. P., Hillhouse, M., & Ling, W. (2012). Hyperalgesia in heroin-dependent patients and the effects of opioid substitution therapy. *Journal of Pain, 13*(4), 401–409.

Compton, P., Kehoe, P., Sinha, K., Torrington, M. A., & Ling, W. (2010). Gabapentin improves cold-pressor pain responses in methadone-maintained patients. *Drug & Alcohol Dependence, 109*(1), 213–219.

Corey, G., Corey, M., & Callanan, P. (1998). *Issues and ethics in the helping professions*. Pacific Grove, CA: Brooks/Cole.

Corte, C., & Becherer, M. (2007). Differential effects of maternal and paternal alcoholism and gender on drinking, alcohol-related self-cognition, and psychopathology. *Journal of Addictions Nursing, 18*(4), 175–185. doi:10.1080/10884600701698828

Crothers, C. E., & Dorrian, J. (2011). Determinants of nurses' attitudes toward the care of patients with alcohol problems. *ISRN Nursing, 2011*. doi:10.5402/2011/821514

Department of Veterans Affairs. (2009). *Substance use disorders VA/ DoD clinical practice guidelines.* Office of Quality and Performance, Department of Veterans Affairs. Available at http://www.healthquality. va.gov/Substance_Use_Disorder_SUD.asp

Desy, P. M., Howard, P. K., Perhats, C., & Li, S. (2010). Alcohol screening, brief intervention, and referral to treatment conducted by emergency nurses: An impact evaluation. *Journal of Emergency Nursing, 36*(6), 538–545.

Desy, P. M., & Perhats, C. (2008). Alcohol screening, brief intervention, and referral in the emergency department: An implementation study. *Journal of Emergency Nursing, 34*(1), 11–19.

Donovan, D. M., & Floyd, A. S. (2008). Facilitating involvement in twelve-step programs. *Recent Developments in Alcoholism, 18*, 303–320.

Dougherty, P. A. (2007). Research synthesis: Adolescent suicide and substance abuse in the United States, 1990–2002. *Journal of Addictions Nursing, 18*(2), 81–91. doi:10.1080/10884600701334853

Duffy, S. A., Essenmacher, C., Karvonen-Gutierrez, C., & A. Ewing, L. (2010). Motivation to quit smoking among veterans diagnosed with psychiatric and substance abuse disorders. *Journal of Addictions Nursing, 21*(2–3), 105–113. doi:10.3109/10884601003777638

Emergency Nurses Association. (2009). *Position Statement: Alcohol screening, brief interventions, and referral to treatment.* Retrieved from http://www.ena.org/SiteCollectionDocuments/Position%20Statements/ Alcohol_Screening_and_Brief_Intervention_-_ENA_PS.pdf

Fabrey, L. J., & Irwin, Z. (2012). *A role delineation study of the addictions nurse and advanced practice addictions nurse.* Olathe, KS: Applied Measurement Professionals, Inc.

Fahy, P., Croton, G., & Voogt, S. (2011). Embedding routine alcohol screening and brief interventions in a rural general hospital. *Drug & Alcohol Review, 30*, 47–54.

Finfgeld-Connett, D., & Madsen, R. (2008). Web-based treatment of alcohol problems among rural women: Results of a randomized pilot investigation. *Journal of Psychosocial Nursing & Mental Health Services, 46*(9), 46.

Finnell, D. S. (2000). The case for teaching patients about the neurobiological basis of addictions. *Journal of Addictions Nursing, 12*(3/4), 149–158.

Finnell, D. S. (2012). A clarion call for nurse-led SBIRT across the continuum of care. *Alcoholism: Clinical & Experimental Research, 36*(7), 1134–1138.

Finnell, D. S., Garbin, M., & Scarborough, J. (2004). Advanced practice addictions nursing specialty certification. *Journal of Addictions Nursing, 15*(1), 37–40.

Finnell, D. S. & Nowzari, S. (2013). Providing information about the neurobiology of alcohol use disorders to close the "referral to treatment gap." *Nursing Clinics of North America, 48*, 373–38. doi:10.1016/j.cnur.2013.04.004

Fiore, M., Bailey, W., Cohen, S., Dorfman, S., & Goldstein, M. (2000). *Treating tobacco use and dependence: A clinical practice guideline.* Rockville, MD: U.S. Department of Health and Human Services, Public Health Services.

Fogger, S. A., & McGuinness, T. (2009). Alabama's nurse monitoring programs: The nurse's experience of being monitored. *Journal of Addictions Nursing, 20*(3), 142–149. doi:10.1080/10884600903078928

Fornili, K., & Burda, C. (2010). Overview of current federal policy for substance use disorders. *Journal of Addictions Nursing, 21*(4), 247–251.

Freeman, S. M. (2004). The relationship of opioid treatment in chronic pain conditions: Implications on brain reward response. *Journal of Addictions Nursing, 15*(1), 3–10. doi:10.1080/jan.15.1.3.10

Gibson, S. (2001). Utilizing empowerment theory in clinical practice with female substance abusers. *Journal of Addictions Nursing, 13*(3–4), 215–221. doi:10.3109/10884600109052656

Gnadt, B. (2006). Religiousness, current substance use, and early risk indicators for substance abuse in nursing students. *Journal of Addictions Nursing, 17*(3), 151–158. doi:10.1080/10884600600862103

Gordon, S. M., Hagan, T. A., Beyer, E., & Snyderman, R. (2001). Eating disorders prevalent for female chemical dependence patients. *Journal of Addictions Nursing, 13*(3–4), 209–214. doi:10.3109/10884600109052655

Gordon-Lamoureux, R. J. (2007). Exploring the possibility of sexual addiction in men arrested for seeking out prostitutes: A preliminary study. *Journal of Addictions Nursing, 18*(1), 21–29. doi:10.1080/10884600601174458

Griffin, V., Musson, P., Allen, K., & Cole-Kissinger, E. (2007). *Living free: Finding freedom from habits that hurt*. Tecumseh, MI: Hamblin Printing.

Groves, P., Pick, S., Davis, P., Cloudesley, R. C. R., Forsythe, M., & Pilling, S. (2011). Routine alcohol screening and brief interventions in general hospital in-patient wards: Acceptability and barriers. *Drugs: Education, Prevention, & Policy, 17*(1), 55–71.

Grupp, K. (2004). Enhancing nurse assessment of alcohol and drug dependency: A preliminary study. *Journal of Addictions Nursing, 15*(2), 81–84. doi:10.1080/10884600490450236

Grupp, K. (2006). Women one year following gender-specific treatment for alcohol and/or other drug dependency. *Journal of Addictions Nursing, 17*(1), 5–11. doi:10.1080/10884600500521817

Grupp, K. (2008). Women with co-occurring substance abuse disorders and PTSD: How women understand their illness. *Journal of Addictions Nursing, 19*(2), 49–54. doi:10.1080/10884600802111697

Haack, M. R., Burda-Cohee, C., Alemi, F., Harge, A., & Nemes, S. (2005). Facilitating self-management of substance use disorders with online counseling: The intervention and study design. *Journal of Addictions Nursing, 16*(1–2), 41–46. doi:10.1080/10884600590917183

Hart, V. A. (2001). Psychotherapy in the age of the computer: The debate concerning computer addiction. *Journal of Addictions Nursing, 13*(3–4), 143–148. doi:10.3109/10884600109052649

Heise, B. (2003). The historical context of addiction in the nursing profession: 1850–1982. *Journal of Addictions Nursing, 14*(3), 117–124. doi:10.1080/jan.14.3.117.124

Hendershot, C. S., Witkiewitz, K., George, W. H., & Marlatt, G. A. (2011). Relapse prevention for addictive behaviors. *Substance Abuse Treatment, Prevention, & Policy, 6*, 1–17. Retrieved from http://www.substanceabusepolicy.com/content/6/1/17

Higgins-Biddle, J., Hungerford, D., & Cates-Wessel, K. (2009). *Screening and brief interventions (SBI) for unhealthy alcohol use: A step-by-step implementation guide for trauma centers.* Atlanta, GA: Centers for Disease Control and Prevention, National Center for Injury Prevention and Control.

Ho, V., Arbour, S., & Hambley, J. M. (2011). Eating disorders and addiction: Comparing eating disorder treatment outcomes among clients with and without comorbid substance use disorder. *Journal of Addictions Nursing, 22*(3), 130–137. doi:10.3109/10884602.2011.585721

Hoxmark, E. M., & Wynn, R. (2010). Health providers' descriptions of the significance of the therapeutic relationship in treatment of patients with dual diagnoses. *Journal of Addictions Nursing, 21*(4), 187–193. doi:10.3109/10884602.2010.520170

Huang, C. M., Chien, L. Y., Cheng, C. F., & Guo, J. L. (2012). Integrating life skills into a theory-based drug-use prevention program: Effectiveness among junior high students in Taiwan. *Journal of School Health, 82*(7), 328–335.

Hughes, R. (2001). CE Feature: Drug injecting and infection-related risk behavior. *Journal of Addictions Nursing, 13*(3–4), 163–174. doi:10.3109/10884600109052651

Hughes, T., McCabe, S. E., Wilsnack, S. C., West, B. T., & Boyd, C. J. (2010). Victimization and substance use disorders in a national sample of heterosexual and sexual minority women and men. *Addiction, 105*(12), 2130–2140.

Inman, R. D., & Kornegay, K. (2004). Exploring the lived experience of surviving with both alcoholism and diabetes. *Journal of Addictions Nursing, 15*(2), 65–72. doi:10.1080/10884600490450218

Institute of Medicine (IOM). (1997). *Managing managed care: Quality improvements in behavioral health.* Washington, DC: National Academies Press.

Institute of Medicine (IOM). (2011). *The future of nursing: Leading change, advancing health.* Washington, DC: National Academies Press.

Institute of Medicine (IOM) Prevention Model. (1997). *Drug abuse prevention: What works.* Rockville, MD: National Institute of Drug Abuse.

International Nurses Society on Addictions (IntNSA). (2006). *Learning from each other: A global perspective of addictions.* Raleigh, NC: Author.

International Nurses Society on Addictions (IntNSA). (2007). *The core curriculum of addictions nursing.* Raleigh, NC: Author.

Jewell, C. E., Tomlinson, J., & Weaver, M. (2011). Identification and management of prescription opioid abuse in hospitalized patients. *Journal of Addictions Nursing, 22*(1–2), 32–38. doi:10.3109/10884602.2010. 545094

Karatay, G., Kublay, G., & Emiroğlu, O. N. (2010). Effect of motivational interviewing on smoking cessation in pregnant women. *Journal of Advanced Nursing, 66*(6), 1328–1337.

Kelly, J. F., Stout, R. L., Magill, M., Tonigan, J. S., & Pagano, M. E. (2011). Spirituality in recovery: A lagged mediational analysis of Alcoholics Anonymous' principal theoretical mechanism of behavior change. *Alcoholism: Clinical & Experimental Research, 35*(3), 454–463.

Kornegay, K., Bugle, L., Jackson, E., & Rives, K. (2004). Facing a problem of great concern: Nursing faculty's lived experience of encounters with chemically dependent nursing students. *Journal of Addictions Nursing, 15*(3), 125–132. doi:10.1080/10884600490491222

Kulbok, P. A., Bovbjerg, V., Meszaros, P. S., Botchwey, N., Hinton, I., Anderson, N. L. R., . . . Hartman, K. (2010). Mother-daughter communication: A protective factor for nonsmoking among rural adolescents. *Journal of Addictions Nursing, 21*(2–3), 69–78. doi:10.3109/10884601003777604

Lawson, L., Conners, N. A., & Crone, C. (2001). Changing the child abuse potential of substance abusing pregnant and parenting women. *Journal of Addictions Nursing, 13*(3–4), 137–142. doi:10.3109/10884600109052648

LeDoux, J. (2002). *Synaptic self.* New York: Penguin.

Lemaire, G. S., Mallik, K., & Rever, K. (2004). Factors influencing community-based rehabilitation for persons with co-occurring psychiatric and substance abuse disorders. *Journal of Addictions Nursing, 15*(1), 15–22. doi:10.1080/10884600490279381

Lewis, M. W. (2001). Facilitation of maternalfetal bonding in pregnant substance-abusing women attending outpatient treatment. *Journal of Addictions Nursing, 13*(3–4), 175–185. doi:10.3109/10884600109052652

Lock, C. A., Kaner, E., Heather, N., Doughty, J., Crawshaw, A., McNamee, P., Purdy, S., & Pearson, P. (2006). Effectiveness of nurse-led brief alcohol intervention: A cluster randomized controlled trial. *Journal of Advanced Nursing, 54*(4), 426–439.

Lowe, J. (2003). The self-reliance of the Cherokee male adolescent. *Journal of Addictions Nursing, 14*(4), 209–214. doi:10.1080/jan.14.4.209.214

Lowe, J., Liang, H., Riggs, C., Henson, J., & Elder, T. (2012). Community partnership to affect substance abuse among Native American adolescents. *American Journal of Drug & Alcohol Abuse, 38*(5), 450–455.

Mamili, M., & Lüscher, C. (2011). Synaptic plasticity and addiction: Learning mechanisms gone awry. *Neuropharmacology, 61*(7), 1052–1059.

Mangold, F. T., Sommers, M. S., Kent, G., & Fargo, J. (2008). Harmful drinking, depression, and conduct disorder among females involved in alcohol-related motor vehicle crashes: A secondary analysis. *Journal of Addictions Nursing, 19*(1), 9–15. doi:10.1080/10884600801896967

Marcus, M. T., Savage, C., & Finnell, D. S. (in press). Nursing roles in addressing addiction. In R. Ries, D. Fiellin, S. Miller, & R. Saitz (Eds.), *Principles of addiction medicine* (5th ed.). Philadelphia, PA: Lippincott Williams & Wilkins.

Marlatt, G. A., & Witkiewitz, K. (2010). Update on harm-reduction policy and intervention research. *Annual Review of Clinical Psychology, 67*(6), 591–606.

Masters, C., & Carlson, D. S. (2006). The process of reconnecting: Recovery from the perspective of addicted women. *Journal of Addictions Nursing, 17*(4), 205–210. doi:10.1080/10884600600995200

McCabe, S. E., Hughes, T. L., Bostwick, W. B., West, B. T., & Boyd, C. J. (2009). Sexual orientation, substance use behaviors and substance dependence in the United States. *Addiction, 104*(8), 1333–1345.

Meyer, B. M. (2009). The Food and Drug Administration Amendments Act of 2007: Drug safety and health-system pharmacy implications. *American Journal of Health-System Pharmacy, 66* (Supp. 7), 53–55.

Miller, A. S. (2005). CE Feature: Adolescent alcohol and substance abuse in rural areas: How telehealth can provide treatment solutions. *Journal of Addictions Nursing, 16*(3), 107–115. doi:10.1080/10884600500196701

Miller, W. R., & Rollnick, S. (2002). *Motivational interviewing: Preparing people for change.* New York: Guilford Press.

Molander, R. C., Yonker, J. A, & Krahn, D. D. (2010). Age-related changes in drinking patterns from mid- to older age: Results from the Wisconsin longitudinal study. *Alcoholism: Clinical & Experimental Research, 34*(7), 1182–1192.

Mollica, M. A., Hyman, Z., & Mann, C. M. (2011). Alcohol-related content in undergraduate nursing curricula in the northeastern United States. *Journal of Psychosocial Nursing, 49*(6), 22–31.

Monroe, T., Pearson, F., & Kenaga, H. (2008). Procedures for handling cases of substance abuse among nurses: A comparison of disciplinary and alternative programs. *Journal of Addictions Nursing, 19*(3), 156–161.

Moore, R. S. (2001). Alternatives to alcohol in coping with workplace stress: Evidence from urban hospital nurses. *Journal of Addictions Nursing, 13*(1), 31–40. doi:10.3109/10884600109087396

Morgan, B. D., & White, D. M. (2009). Managing pain in patients with co-occurring addictive disorders. *Journal of Addictions Nursing, 20*(1), 41–48. doi:10.1080/10884600802694809

Murray, M. M., & Savage, C. (2010). The NIAAA BSN nursing education curriculum: A rationale and overivew. *Journal of Addictions Nursing, 21*(1), 3–5.

Musayón, Y., Alayo, M., Loncharich, N., & Armstrong, M. (2008). Factors associated with alcohol consumption in schoolgirls in a school in Lima, Peru. *Journal of Addictions Nursing, 19*(4), 188–194. doi:10.1080/10884600802504859

Nakhaee, N., & Jadidi, N. (2009). Why do some teens turn to drugs? A focus group study of drug users' experiences. *Journal of Addictions Nursing, 20*(4), 203–208. doi:10.3109/10884600903291158

National Abandoned Infants Recource Center. (2008). Women with co-occurring mental illness and substance abuse. *Journal of Addictions Nursing, 19*(2), 93–100. doi:10.1080/10884600802111655

National Center for Biotechnology Information. (2004). A science primer: One size does not fit all: The promise of pharmacogenomics. Retrieved from http://www.ncbi.nlm.nih.gov/About/primer/pharm.html

National Institute on Alcohol Abuse and Alcoholism (NIAAA). (2007). *Helping patients who drink too much: A clinician's guide* (2nd ed.). Rockville, MD: U.S. Department of Health and Human Services.

National Institute on Alcohol Abuse and Alcoholism (NIAAA). (2008). Alcohol and other drugs. *Alcohol Alert, 76*, 1–4.

National Institute on Drug Abuse (NIDA). (2012). *Screening for drug use in general medical settings.* Rockville, MD: U.S. Department of Health and Human Services. Available at http://www.drugabuse.gov/publications/resource-guide

National Nurses Society on Addictions & American Nurses Association. (1989). *Standards of addiction nursing practice with selected diagnoses and criteria.* Kansas City, MO: American Nurses Association.

National Quality Forum. (2007). National voluntary consensus standards for the treatment of substance use conditions: Evidence-based treatment practices. Washington, DC: National Quality Forum.

Neil-Urban, S., Lasala, K. B., & Scott, L. (2001). The state of smoking cessation practices among health care providers: Educational preparation and motivating factors presented. *Journal of Addictions Nursing, 13*(1), 9–18. doi:10.3109/10884600109087394

Nitzkin, J. L., & Smith, S. A. (2004). Clinical preventive services in substance abuse and mental health update: From science to services (DHHS Publication No. (SMA) 04-3906). Washington, DC: Substance Abuse and Mental Health Services Administration.

O'Brien, C. (2011). Addiction and dependence in *DSM-V. Addiction, 106*(5), 866–867.

Oddie, S., & Davies, J. (2009). A multi-method evaluation of a substance misuse program in a medium secure forensic mental health unit. *Journal of Addictions Nursing, 20*(3), 132–141. doi:10.1080/10884600903078944

Office of the Federal Registrar. (2003). *Code of Federal Regulations. Title 42: Public Health, Part 2. Confidentiality of alcohol and drug abuse patient records.* Available at: URL: http://www.bookstore.gpo.gov

Oliver, J., Coggins, C., Compton, P., Hagan, S., Matteliano, D., Stanton, M., St. Marie, B., Strobbe, S., & Turner, H. N. (2012). American Society for Pain Management Nursing position statement: Pain management in patients with substance use disorders. *Journal of Addictions Nursing, 23*(3), 210–222.

Orman, J. S., & Keating, G. M. (2009). Buprenorphine/naloxone. *Drugs, 69*(5), 577–607.

Osterman, R. (2011). Feasibility of using motivational interviewing to decrease alcohol consumption during pregnancy. *Journal of Addictions Nursing, 22*(3), 93–102. doi:10.3109/10884602.2011.585723

Owens, L., Butcher, G., Gilmore, I., et al. (2011). A randomised controlled trial of extended brief intervention for alcohol dependent patients in an acute hospital setting (ADPAC). *BMC Public Health, 11,* 528.

Parker, F. M., Faulk, D., & LoBello, S. G. (2003). Assessing codependency and family pathology in nursing students. *Journal of Addictions Nursing, 14*(2), 85–90. doi:10.1080/10884600390230484

Payne, L. G. (2010). Self-acceptance and its role in women's recovery from addiction. *Journal of Addictions Nursing, 21*(4), 207–214. doi:10.3109/10884602.2010.515693

Pillon, S. C., Ramos, L. H., Villar-Luis, M. A., & Rassool, G. H. (2004). Nursing students' perceptions of the curricula content on drug and alcohol education in Brazil: An exploratory study. *Journal of Addictions Nursing, 15,* 133–137.

Potter, E., Cashin, A., Andriotis, H., & Rosina, R. (2008). Examining the role of nursing in (youth) drug court programs. *Journal of Addictions Nursing, 19*(4), 182–187. doi:10.1080/10884600802505070

Pray, M. E., & Watson, L. M. (2008). Effectiveness of day treatment for dual-diagnosis patients with severe chronic mental illness. *Journal of Addictions Nursing, 19*(3), 141–149. doi:10.1080/10884600802306008

Puskar, K. R., Bernardo, L. M., Switala, J., & Chughtai, R. L. (2008). Adolescent substance use in rural America: Current profile. *Journal of Addictions Nursing, 19*(3), 150–155. doi:10.1080/10884600802306123

Ragaisis, K. M. (2004). Alcohol screening in the acute care hospital. *Journal of Addictions Nursing, 15*(4), 171–175. doi:10.1080/10884600490889294

Rassool, G. H. (2006). Substance abuse in Black and minority ethnic communities in the United Kingdom: A neglected problem? *Journal of Addictions Nursing, 17*(2), 127–132. doi:10.1080/10884600600668443

Rassool, G. H., & Villar-Luís, M. (2006). Reproductive risks of alcohol and illicit drugs: An overview. *Journal of Addictions Nursing, 17*(4), 211–213. doi:10.1080/10884600600995242

Ratey, J. (2002). *A user's guide to the brain.* New York: Vintage Books.

Robinson, R. (2006). Health perceptions and health-related quality of life of substance abusers: A review of the literature. *Journal of Addictions Nursing, 17*(3), 159–168. doi:10.1080/10884600600862137

Roche, A. M., Pidd, K., & Freeman, T. (2009). Achieving professional practice change: From training to workforce development. *Drug & Alcohol Review, 28,* 550–557. doi:10.111/j.1465-3362.2009.0011x

Roller, C. G. (2004). Sex addiction and women: A nursing issue. *Journal of Addictions Nursing, 15*(2), 53–61. doi:10.1080/10884600490450263

Saarnio, P., & Knuuttila, V. (2007). A study of readiness to change profiles in alcohol and other drug abusers. *Journal of Addictions Nursing, 18*(3), 117–122. doi:10.1080/10884600701500602

Santisteban, D. A., Mena, M. P., & McCabe, B. E. (2011). Preliminary results for an adaptive family treatment for drug abuse in Hispanic youth. *Journal of Family Psychology, 25*(4), 610.

Savage, C. L. (2008). Pharmacotherapy for alcohol dependence: Medical management and the role of nursing. *Journal of Addictions Nursing, 19*(3), 170–171.

Savage, C. L., Dyehouse, J., Marcus, M., & Lindell, A. (2011). Alcohol and health content in baccalaureate nursing programs. *Alcoholism: Clinical & Experimental Research, 35*(6S), 254.

Savage, C. L., & Wray, J. N. (2004). Family history of alcohol use as predictor of alcohol and tobacco use during pregnancy. *Journal of Addictions Nursing, 15*(3), 119–123. doi:10.1080/10884600490491213

Shen, X. Y., Orson, F. M., & Kosten, T. R. (2012). Vaccines against drug abuse. *Clinical Pharmacology & Therapeutics, 91*(1), 60–70.

Smith, P. C., Schmidt, S. M., Allensworth-Davies, D., & Saitz, R. (2010). A single-question screening test for drug use in primary care. *Archives of Internal Medicine, 170*(13), 1155.

Snow, D., Smith, T., & Branham, S. (2008). Women with bipolar disorder who use alcohol and other drugs. *Journal of Addictions Nursing, 19*(2), 55–60. doi:10.1080/10884600802111739

Snow, D., & Trowbridge, L. (2010). Predictors of alcohol abuse in college-age drinkers: The role of family history. *Journal of Addictions Nursing, 21*(4), 238–241. doi:10.3109/10884602.2010.525838

Sobczak, J. A. (2009). Alcohol use and sexual function in women: A literature review. *Journal of Addictions Nursing, 20*(2), 71–85. doi:10.1080/10884600902850095

Stanley, K. M., Worrall, C. L., Lunsford, S. L., Couillard, D. J., & Norcross, E. D. (2007). Efficacy of a symptom-triggered practice guideline for managing alcohol withdrawal syndrome in an academic medical center. *Journal of Addictions Nursing, 18*(4), 207–216. doi:10.1080/10884600701699255

Staton, M., Walker, R., & Leukefeld, C. (2003). Age differences in risk behavior among incarcerated substance-abusing women. *Journal of Addictions Nursing, 14*(1), 3–9. doi:10.1080/10884600305365

Strobbe, S., Perhats, C., & Broyles, L. M. (in press). [A joint position paper on behalf of the International Nurses Society on Addictions (IntNSA) and the Emergency Nurses Association]. Expanded roles and responsibilities for nurses in screening, brief intervention, and referral to treatment (SBIRT) for alcohol use. *Journal of Addictions Nursing.*

Strobbe, S., Cranford, J. A., Wojnar, M., & Brower, K. J. (in press). [Special issue: Spirituality and addiction]. *Journal of Addictions Nursing.*

Strobbe, S., Hagerty, B., & Boyd, C. (2012). Applying the nursing Theory of Human Relatedness to alcoholism and recovery in Alcoholics Anonymous. *Journal of Addictions Nursing, 23*(4), 241–247.

Strobbe, S., & Hobbins, D. (2012). The prescribing of buprenorphine by advanced practice registered nurses. *Journal of Addictions Nursing, 23*(1), 82–83.

Strobbe, S., Mathias, L., Gibbons, P. W., Humenay, E., & Brower, K. J. (2011). Buprenorphine clinic for opioid maintenance therapy: Program description, process measures, and patient satisfaction. *Journal of Addictions Nursing, 22*(1–2), 8–12. doi:10.3109/10884602.2010.545090

Substance Abuse and Mental Health Services Administration (SAMHSA). (2011). *Results from the 2010 National Survey on Drug Use and Health: Summary of national findings* (NSDUH Series H-41, HHS Publication No. (SMA) 11-4658). Rockville, MD: Author.

Substance Abuse and Mental Health Services Administration (SAMHSA). (2012). *Results from the 2011 National Survey on Drug Use and Health: Summary of national findings* (NSDUH Series H-44, HHS Publication No. (SMA) 12-4713). Rockville, MD: Author.

Suissa, A. J. (2007). Gambling addiction as a pathology: Some markers for empowerment. *Journal of Addictions Nursing, 18*(2), 93–101. doi:10.1080/10884600701334952

Sullivan, E., & Fleming, M. (1997). *TIP 24: A guide to substance abuse services for primary care clinicians* (DHHS Publication No. (SMA) 97-3139). Rockville, MD: U.S. Department of Health and Human Services, Substance Abuse and Mental Health Services Administration.

Sussman, S., Lisha, N., & Griffiths, M. (2011). Prevalence of the addictions: A problem of the majority or minority? *Evaluation & the Health Professions, 34*(1), 3–56. doi:10.1177/0163278710380124 [Epub September 27, 2010.]

Urbanoski, K. A., & Kelly, J. F. (2012). Understanding genetic risk for substance use and addiction: A guide for non-geneticists. *Clinical Psychology Review, 32*, 60–70.

U.S. Department of Health and Human Services (U.S. DHHS). (2009a). *Principles of drug addiction treatment: A research-based guide* (NIH Publication No. 09-4180). Rockville, MD: Author.

U.S. Department of Health and Human Services (U.S. DHHS). (2012). *Screening for drug use in general medical settings: Resource guide.* Rockville, MD: National Institute of Drug Abuse. Available at http://www.drugabuse.gov/sites/default/files/resource_guide.pdf

U.S. Department of Health and Human Services (U.S. DHHS). (2011). *Substance abuse.* Retrieved from http://healthypeople.gov/2020/topicsobjectives2020/overview.aspx?topicid=40

U.S. Food and Drug Administration (FDA). (2013) Risk Evaluation and Mitigation Strategy (REMS) for Extended-Release and Long-Acting Opioids. Retrieved from http://www.fda.gov/Drugs/DrugSafety/InformationbyDrugClass/ucm163647.htm

U.S. Preventive Services Task Force. (2004). *Screening and behavioral counseling interventions in primary care to reduce alcohol misuse.* Rockville, MD: Agency for Healthcare Research and Quality. Available at http://www.uspreventiveservicestaskforce.org/uspstf/uspsdrin.htm

U.S. Preventive Services Task Force. (2008). *Screening for illicit drug use: Recommendation statement* (AHRQ Publication 08-05108-EF-3). Rockville, MD: Agency for Healthcare Research and Quality. Available at http://www.uspreventiveservicestaskforce.org/uspstf08/druguse/drugrs.pdf

Vandermause, R. K. (2007). Assessing for alcohol use disorders in women: Experiences of advanced practice nurses in primary care settings. *Journal of Addictions Nursing, 18*(4), 187–198. doi:10.1080/10884600701699347

Varela, T. A., Montbach, J., & Shipe, S. (2007). Psychoactive medication adherence in substance users living with HIV/AIDS. *Journal of Addictions Nursing, 18*(1), 5–12. doi:10.1080/10884600601174409

Venios, K., & Kelly, J. F. (2010). The rise, risks, and realities of methamphetamine use among women: Implications for research, prevention and treatment. *Journal of Addictions Nursing, 21*(1), 14–21. doi:10.3109/10884601003628120

Vocci, F. J., Acri, J., & Elkashef, A. (2005). Medication development for addictive disorders: The state of the science. *American Journal of Psychiatry, 162*(8), 1432–1440.

Voyer, P., Préville, M., Martin, L. S., Roussel, M.-E., Béland, S.-G., & Berbiche, D. (2011). Factors associated with self-rated benzodiazepine addiction among community-dwelling seniors. *Journal of Addictions Nursing, 22*(1–2), 46–56. doi:10.3109/10884602.2010.545087

Wilson, H., & Compton, M. (2009). Reentry of the addicted certified registered nurse anesthetist: A review of the literature. *Journal of Addictions Nursing, 20*(4), 177–184. doi:10.3109/10884600903078951

Witbrodt, J., Kaskutas, L. A., Diehl, S., Armstrong, M. A., Escobar, G. J., Taillac, C., & Osejo, V. (2007). Using drink size to talk about drinking during pregnancy: Early Start Plus. *Journal of Addictions Nursing, 18*(4), 199–206. doi:10.1080/10884600701699420

World Health Organization (WHO). (2004). *International statistical classification of diseases and related health problems.* Geneva, Switzerland: Author.

World Health Organization (WHO). (2011a). *The global status report on alcohol and health.* Geneva, Switzerland: Author.

World Health Organization (WHO). (2011b). *Management of substance abuse.* Geneva, Switzerland: Author. Retrieved from http://www.who.int /substance_abuse/terminology/definition2/en/index.html

World Health Organization (WHO). (2011c). Tobacco free initiative. Geneva, Switzerland: Author. Available at http://www.who.int/tobacco/ health_priority/en/

Wu, S. M., Compton, P., Bolus, R., Schieffer, B., Pham, Q., Baria, A.,… & Naliboff, B. D. (2006). The addiction behaviors checklist: Validation of a new clinician-based measure of inappropriate opioid use in chronic pain. *Journal of Pain & Symptom Management, 32*(4), 342–351.

Young, C., & Kornegay, K. (2004). Understanding why health care professionals continue to smoke. *Journal of Addictions Nursing, 15*(1), 31–35. doi:10.1080/jan.15.1.31.35

Appendix A.

Scope and Standards of Addictions Nursing Practice (2004)

Scope and Standards of Addictions Nursing Practice

International Nurses Society on Addictions

American Nurses Association

The content in this appendix is not current and is of historical significance only.

SCOPE AND STANDARDS
OF ADDICTIONS
NURSING PRACTICE

Washington, D.C.
2004

International Nurses
Society on Addictions

The content in this appendix is not current and is of historical significance only.

Acknowledgements

The International Nurses Society on Addictions (IntNSA) is grateful to the following individuals who have put their time, energy, and commitment into the completion of this revised 2003 version of the *Scope and Standards of Addictions Nursing*. IntNSA wishes to thank the ANA for its contributions to the completion of this important document and the support of the IntNSA Board of Directors.

Editors/Chairs of Revision
Karen Allen, PhD, RN, FAAN, Andrews University
Diane Snow, PhD, APRN, BC, CARN, PMHNP, University of Texas at Arlington
*Lynette Jack, PhD, RN, CARN, University of Pittsburgh

Other contributors and reviewers
Merry Armstrong, DNSc, MS, ARNP
 Carolyn Baird, MEd, RNC-PMH, CARN-AP, CAAP
*Kathleen Ballard, MSN, RN
*Cass Breslin, RN
 Janice Feigenbaum, PhD, RN
*Kathleen Flanagan, RN
*Kem Louie, PhD, RN, APRN, BC, FAAN
*Connie Mele, MSN, RN, CARN-AP
 Dana Murphy Parker, MS, RN
 Christine Savage, Ph.D, RN
*Eleanor Sullivan, PhD, RN, FAAN
 *Lynn Swisher, PhD, RN
*Nancy Fisk, MSN, RN
*Patricia Rowell, PhD, RN

Members of original revision workgroup.

Addictions Nursing: Scope and Standards of Practice

The content in this appendix is not current and is of historical significance only.

CONTENTS

The content in this appendix is not current and is of historical significance only.

The content in this appendix is not current and is of historical significance only.

PRACTICE STANDARDS FOR ADDICTIONS NURSING: STANDARDS OF CARE

STANDARD 1. ASSESSMENT

The addictions nurse collects patient health data.

STANDARD 2. DIAGNOSIS

The addictions nurse analyzes the assessment data in determining diagnoses.

STANDARD 3. OUTCOME IDENTIFICATION

The addictions nurse identifies expected outcomes individualized to the patient.

STANDARD 4. PLANNING

The addictions nurse develops an individualized plan of care that prescribes interventions to attain expected outcomes.

STANDARD 5. IMPLEMENTATION

The addictions nurse implements the interventions identified in the plan of care.

STANDARD 5A. THERAPEUTIC ALLIANCE

The addictions nurse uses the "therapeutic self" to establish a therapeutic alliance with the patient and to structure nursing interventions to promote development of insight, coping skills, and motivation for change in behavior that promotes health.

STANDARD 5B. HEALTH TEACHING

The addictions nurse, through health teaching, assists individuals, families, groups, and communities in achieving satisfying, productive, and healthy patterns of living.

STANDARD 5C. SELF-CARE AND SELF-MANAGEMENT

The addictions nurse uses the knowledge and philosophy of self-care and self-management to assist the patient in learning new ways to address stress, maintain self-control, accept personal responsibility, and integrate healthy coping behaviors into life-style choices.

STANDARD 5D. PHARMACOLOGICAL, BIOLOGICAL, AND COMPLEMENTARY THERAPIES

The addictions nurse applies knowledge of pharmacological, biological, and complementary therapies and uses clinical skills to restore the patient's health and prevent consequences from addiction.

STANDARD 5E. THERAPEUTIC MILIEU

The addictions nurse structures, provides, and maintains a therapeutic environment in collaboration with the patient and other healthcare providers.

STANDARD 5F. COUNSELING

The addictions nurse uses counseling interventions to assist patients in promoting healthy coping abilities, preventing addiction, and addressing issues related to patterns of abuse and addiction.

STANDARD 6. EVALUATION

The addictions nurse evaluates the patient's progress toward attainment of expected outcomes.

PRACTICE STANDARDS
FOR ADDICTIONS NURSING:
STANDARDS OF PROFESSIONAL PERFORMANCE

STANDARD 7. QUALITY OF CARE

The addictions nurse systematically evaluates the quality of care and effectiveness of nursing practice.

STANDARD 8. PERFORMANCE APPRAISAL

The addictions nurse evaluates his or her own nursing practice in relation to professional practice standards and relevant statutes and regulations.

STANDARD 9. EDUCATION

The addictions nurse acquires and maintains current knowledge and competency in nursing practice.

STANDARD 10. COLLEGIALITY

The addictions nurse interacts with and contributes to the professional development of peers, and treats other healthcare providers as colleagues.

STANDARD 11. ETHICS

The nurse's decisions and actions on behalf of patients are determined and implemented in an ethical manner.

STANDARD 12. COLLABORATION

The nurse collaborates with the patient, significant others, and other healthcare providers in providing patient care.

STANDARD 13. RESEARCH

The addictions nurse uses theory and evidence from research findings to guide practice.

STANDARD 14. RESOURCE UTILIZATION

The addictions nurse considers factors related to safety, effectiveness, and cost in planning and delivering patient care.

The content in this appendix is not current and is of historical significance only.

ADVANCED PRACTICE STANDARDS FOR ADDICTIONS NURSING: STANDARDS OF CARE

STANDARD 1. ASSESSMENT

The advanced practice addictions registered nurse collects comprehensive patient health data.

STANDARD 2. DIAGNOSIS

The advanced practice addictions registered nurse critically analyzes the assessment data in determining the diagnoses.

STANDARD 3. OUTCOME IDENTIFICATION

The advanced practice registered nurse identifies expected outcomes derived from the assessment data and diagnoses, and individualizes expected outcomes with the patient and the healthcare team when appropriate.

STANDARD 4. PLANNING

The advanced practice addictions registered nurse develops a comprehensive treatment plan that includes interventions to attain expected outcomes.

STANDARD 5. IMPLEMENTATION

The advanced practice addictions registered nurse prescribes, orders, or implements addictions interventions and treatments for the plan of care.

STANDARD 5A. CASE MANAGEMENT AND COORDINATION OF CARE

The advanced practice addictions registered nurse provides comprehensive clinical coordination of care and case management.

STANDARD 5B. CONSULTATION

The advanced practice addictions registered nurse provides consultation to influence the plan of care for patients, enhance the abilities of others to provide quality care to addicted patients, and effect change in the system.

STANDARD 5C. HEALTH PROMOTION, HEALTH MAINTENANCE, AND HEALTH TEACHING

The advanced practice addictions registered nurse employs complex strategies, interventions, and teaching to promote, maintain, and improve health and prevent illness and injury.

STANDARD 5D. PRESCRIPTIVE AUTHORITY AND TREATMENT

The advanced practice addictions registered nurse uses prescriptive authority, procedures, and treatments in accordance with educational preparation, state and federal laws and regulations, applicable nurse practice acts, and appropriate advanced practice certification to treat illness and improve functional health status or to provide preventive care.

STANDARD 5E. PSYCHOTHERAPY AND COMPLEMENTARY THERAPY

The advanced practice addictions registered nurse conducts individual, group, and family psychotherapy, and educates about and evaluates the use of complementary therapies to promote healthy lifestyles, prevent addictive behaviors, treat addictions and improve health status and functional abilities.

STANDARD 5F. REFERRAL

The advanced practice addictions registered nurse identifies the need for additional care and makes referrals as needed.

STANDARD 6. EVALUATION

The advanced practice addictions registered nurse evaluates the patient's progress in attaining expected outcomes.

The content in this appendix is not current and is of historical significance only.

ADVANCED PRACTICE STANDARDS FOR ADDICTIONS NURSING: STANDARDS OF PROFESSIONAL PERFORMANCE

STANDARD 7. QUALITY OF CARE

The advanced practice addictions registered nurse develops criteria for and evaluates the quality of care and effectiveness of advanced practice addictions registered nurses.

STANDARD 8. SELF-EVALUATION

The advanced practice addictions registered nurse continuously evaluates their nursing practice in relation to professional practice standards and relevant statutes and regulations, and is accountable to the public and to the profession for providing competent clinical care.

STANDARD 9. EDUCATION

The advanced practice addictions registered nurse acquires and maintains current knowledge and skills in addictions practice.

STANDARD 10. LEADERSHIP

The advanced practice addictions registered nurse serves as a leader and a role model for the professional development of peers, colleagues, and others.

STANDARD 11. ETHICS

The advanced practice addictions registered nurse integrates ethical principles and norms in all areas of practice.

STANDARD 12. INTERDISCIPLINARY PROCESS

The advanced practice addictions registered nurse promotes an interdisciplinary process in providing patient care.

STANDARD 13. RESEARCH

The advanced practice addictions registered nurse utilizes theory and research to discover, examine, and evaluate knowledge, theories, and creative approaches to healthcare practice.

The content in this appendix is not current and is of historical significance only.

SCOPE OF PRACTICE
FOR ADDICTIONS NURSING

Introduction

In 1983 the American Nurses Association, the National Nurses Society on Addictions, and the Drug and Alcohol Nurses Association led the effort to delineate the practice of addictions nursing by forming a task force on addictions nursing practice. This resulted in the publication of *Care of Clients with Addictions: Dimensions of Nursing Practice*, which described nursing practice in the prevention and intervention of abuse and addiction of substances and behaviors (American Nurses Association, Drug and Alcohol Nursing Association, & National Nurses Society on Addictions, 1987). In 1989 the *Standards of Addiction Nursing Practice with Selected Diagnoses and Criteria* was published by the National Nurses Society on Addiction and the American Nurses Association. Addictions nursing practice is a distinct specialty that integrates biological, behavioral, environmental, psychological, social, cultural, and spiritual aspects of human responses to the illness of addiction into the nursing care provided to those affected by this disorder/disease, regardless of the clinical setting.

Since that time, significant changes occurring within the healthcare arena have affected addictions nursing practice including:

- Research on the causes and treatment of addictions revealing new insights that affect the care of addicted persons.

- Social and healthcare policy that affects the prevention and treatment of addiction in individuals and populations.

- Healthcare financing and reimbursement that help shape when, where, how, and what kind of care addicted persons receive.

- Graying of the population, which has meant adapting and developing modalities of care that meet the specific needs of older individuals (this includes the need for tools for assessing substance use and abuse).

Like other nursing specialties, the scope of addictions nursing practice continues to evolve. Society's increasing need and demand for nurses with expertise in the treatment and prevention of addictions has broadened the scope of the specialty. As nursing moves toward an evidence-based model of practice, the specialty of addictions nursing is growing in its knowledge about addictions and its development of addictions theories and theories from related disciplines.

The content in this appendix is not current and is of historical significance only.

With the increasing prevalence of substance use disorders and other addictions in all segments of the population, all nurses, regardless of their practice setting, require evidence-based standards of care for their patients affected directly or indirectly by addictions. The specialty of addictions nursing provides leadership to the profession by providing evidence-based standards of care, cutting edge nursing research related to addiction, and forums for developing new and innovative approaches aimed at reducing the prevalence of addiction and increasing the use of effective interventions related to addiction.

Extent of the Addictions Problem

Incidence and Prevalence of Alcohol and Other Drug Addictions

Based on the most recent data from the National Household Survey on Drug Abuse (SAMHSA, 2002, pp. 1–4) in the United States:

- 109 million Americans age 12 years and older reported current use of alcohol, meaning they used alcohol at least once during the 30 days prior to the interview.

- 25.1 million Americans aged 12 years and older reported driving under the influence of alcohol at least once in the 12 months prior to the interview. Approximately 22.8% of young adults age 18 to 25 years drove under the influence of alcohol.

- 10.1 million current drinkers were age 12–20, despite the fact that alcohol consumption is not legal for those Americans under 21 years of age. Of this group, 6.8 million engaged in binge drinking with 2.1 million classified as heavy drinkers.

- An estimated 66.5 million Americans age 12 years and older reported use of a tobacco product during the 30 days prior to the interview.

- Approximately 13.0% of youth age 12 to 17 years used a tobacco product during the 30 days prior to the interview. However, based on the *Monitoring the Future* study, Johnston et al. (2003, p. 42) reported that 31.4% of eighth graders, 47.4% of tenth graders, and 57.2% of twelfth graders had smoked cigarettes at least once in their life.

- An estimated 15.9 million Americans age 12 years and older (7.1 % of this population) used an illicit drug at least once during the 30 days prior to the interview. Approximately 10.8 % of 12- to 17-year-olds and 18.8 % of young adults ages 18 to 25 years used an illicit drug at least once during the 30 days prior to the interview.

The content in this appendix is not current and is of historical significance only.

- Approximately 1.6% of Americans age 12 years and older have engaged in the nonmedical use of pain relievers and 0.6 % have engaged in the nonmedical use of tranquilizers.

- Approximately 8.1 million Americans age 12 and older have tried ecstasy (MDMA) at least once in their life.

- Close to one million (957,000) Americans age 12 years and older reported the use of Oxycontin for a nonmedical purpose.

- An estimated 16.6 million persons age 12 years and older were classified with dependence on or abuse of either alcohol or illicit drugs (7.3 % of the population).

- Based on the *Monitoring the Future* study, Johnston et al. (2003) reported that 24.5% of eighth graders, 44.6% of tenth graders, and 53.0% of twelfth graders in the United States had used an illicit drug at least once in their life. This use included:

  - 19.2% of eighth graders, 38.7% of tenth graders, and 47.8% of twelfth graders had used marijuana or hashish.

  - 15.2% of eighth graders, 13.5% of tenth graders, and 11.7% of twelfth graders had used an inhalant.

  - 4.1% of eighth graders, 7.8% of tenth graders, and 12.0% of twelfth graders had used a hallucinogen.

  - 3.1% of twelfth graders used PCP (phencyclidine).

  - 4.3% of eighth graders, 6.6% of tenth graders, and 10.5% of twelfth graders had used ecstasy (MDMA).

  - 3.6% of eighth graders, 6.1% of tenth graders, and 7.8% of twelfth graders had used cocaine or crack.

  - 1.6% of eighth graders, 1.8% of tenth graders, and 1.7% of twelfth graders had used heroin.

  - 10.1% of twelfth graders had used a narcotic other than heroi.

  - 8.7% of eighth graders, 14.9% of tenth graders, and 16.8% of twelfth graders had used an amphetamine.

  - 3.5% of eighth graders, 6.1% of tenth graders, and 6.7% of twelfth graders had used a methamphetamine.

  - 9.5% of twelfth graders had used a barbiturate.

  - 4.3% of eighth graders, 8.8% of tenth graders, and 11.4% of twelfth graders had used a tranquilizer.

  - 0.8% of eighth graders, and 1.3% of tenth graders had used rohypnol.

The content in this appendix is not current and is of historical significance only.

- The problems of abuse and dependence among the older population are believed to be substantial, but difficult to estimate because of the lack of data and focus on this issue (Korper & Council, 2002).

- Korper and Raskin (Korper & Council, 2002) project a doubling of individuals age 50 years and older with substance abuse problems in the next 20 years.

- An estimated 14.8 million American adults age 18 years or older had a severe mental illness (7.3% of the population). An estimated 3.0 million people, approximately 20.3% of this group, were dependent on or abused alcohol or illicit drugs (SAMHSA, 2002, p. 4).

Incidence and Prevalence of Alcohol and Other Drug Addictions Worldwide

The Global Burden of Disease (GBD), a project of the World Health Organization (WHO) and the World Bank (Murray & Lopez, 1996), highlighted the significance of the burden of mental health and addiction issues by estimating disability rather than more traditional mortality rates. Based on estimates of the Disease Adjusted Life Years (DALYs) in 1990, psychiatric conditions, including substance misuse, accounted for nearly 11% of disease burden worldwide. In the developed regions of the world alcohol use was the leading cause of disability in males and the tenth largest in women. In developing regions alcohol use was the fourth largest cause of disability in men.

Projections for the year 2020 in the GBD include a dramatic rise in deaths from tobacco, which is expected to kill more people than any single disease, and which will surpass the HIV epidemic. From its 1990 level of 2.6% of all disease burdens worldwide, the burden from diseases related to tobacco is expected to be up to 9%. Tobacco is fast becoming a global health emergency.

Violence will rise from 19th place to 12th place, and HIV is expected to be the 10th leading cause of disease burden worldwide by 2020. Closely associated with drug and alcohol use is the number of road traffic accidents, which will rise from 9th to 3rd place in young adults. Unipolar major depression, often a sequela or etiological factor for abuse and addiction, is expected to be the leading cause of disease burden in women and in developing countries, while overall it is projected to be ranked second worldwide, accounting for 5.7% of the disease burden in 2020.

The content in this appendix is not current and is of historical significance only.

Incidence and Prevalence of Other Addictions

According to the National Gambling Impact and Policy Commission (NGIPC) (1999), gambling is an increasingly popular leisure activity enjoyed in the United States by a majority of adults and youth. There is an estimated 1 to 3% prevalence rate of adult problem or pathological gambling, with a 3:1 gender ratio of men to women (APA, 2000). Blume (1997) reported that approximately 4% of adults have some gambling related problems, with a higher rate of 9% for compulsive gambling among those in treatment for addictive substance disorders. Some experts place the problem gambling rate among adolescents to be higher (Adlaf & Ialomiteanu, 2000; Jacobs, 2000) The NGIPC (1999) study estimated that the prevalence rate of pathological gambling of adolescents is approximately 5%, while the rate of problem gambling is approximately 6%.

The prevalence of sexual addiction has been estimated at 3 to 6% of the American population (Goodman, 1997). Many regard eating disorders as food addiction, or the use of food in an addictive behavioral manner to address emotional issues (Blundell & Hill, 1993; David & Claridge, 1998; Pirke, 1990). Approximately 0.5% of women between the ages of 15 and 40 years exhibit anorexia. One to 1.5% of women exhibit symptoms of bulimia (Gold, Johnson, and Stennie, 1997).

Addicted Patients in Clinical Settings

Based on data from the 1998 National Hospital Discharge Survey, Hall and Popovich (2000) reported that approximately 1.5% of discharges from short-stay hospitals gave alcohol-related diagnoses as the first-listed diagnosis. This value would be much higher if tallied from any listed diagnoses. Evaluating alcohol-related discharge diagnoses does not account for conditions such as peptic ulcer disease, burns, fractures, and injuries from automobile accidents that commonly have alcohol as a contributory factor (National Institute on Alcohol Abuse and Alcoholism, 1998). Nurses in other healthcare facilities care for the untold numbers of patients with addictions-related illness resulting from drug abuse/addiction, eating disorders, and lifestyle illnesses, such as HIV/AIDS obtained through addictive behaviors.

Description of Addictions

Definition and Characteristics

In the past ten years researchers, under the auspices of the National Institute on Drug Abuse and the National Institute on Alcohol Abuse and Alcoholism,

The content in this appendix is not current and is of historical significance only.

have repeatedly demonstrated that addiction is a brain disorder/disease. Specific neurochemical processes occurring in the brain are linked to addiction and relapse in individuals attempting to maintain abstinence. The scientific evidence has helped to remove the former belief that individuals with an addiction suffered from a moral deficit or insufficient willpower. What is now known is that the development of an addictive disorder is related to a complex interaction of environmental, social, genetic, psychological, and biological risk factors (Wilcox & Erickson, 2000).

Current research is helping us to understand the mechanism by which exposure to chemicals results in addiction. According to the National Institute on Drug Abuse (1994), prolonged exposure to drugs leads to molecular adaptations in certain proteins found within neurons in the mesocorticolimbic dopamine system—a brain pathway that is important for drug reward and craving. Dopamine, produced from the precursor tyrosine, is dysregulated as the disease progresses. The medial forebrain bundle, comprising the ventral tegmental area, lateral hypothalamus, nucleus accumbens, amygdala, and frontal cortex, is involved in addiction/dependency from the excessive dopamine release. Thus, the person with an addiction has a drive that is "automatic" and outside of conscious control (Wilcox & Erickson, 2000). Other neurotranmsitters involved include serotonin (5HT) and gamma amino butyric acid (GABA). Long-term adaptations in these proteins caused by chronic drug use may contribute to such addictive aspects as: tolerance, sensitization, reinforcement, and the compulsion to continue to achieve a desired effect.

Addiction is an illness characterized by compulsion, loss of control, and continued use despite perceived negative consequences. Types of addictions include alcohol dependence (alcoholism), drug dependence (including nicotine), eating disorders, excessive gambling or spending, and compulsive sexual disorders. Addiction is progressive, but does respond to comprehensive and varied treatment approaches, which foster the patient's active participation and acceptance of responsibility.

Addiction is a complex neurobiobehavioral disorder characterized by impaired control, compulsive use, dependency, and craving for the activity, substance, or food. Relapses are possible even after long periods of abstinence (National Institute on Drug Abuse [NIDA], 2002b; Wilcox & Erickson, 2000). Addiction is often (but not always) accompanied by physiological dependence, consisting of a withdrawal syndrome, or tolerance (NIDA, 2002a). Factors contributing to the development of addiction include genetic predisposition, the reinforcing properties and access to the substance, food, or activity, family and peer influences, sociocultural environment, personality, and existing psychiatric disorders (Goldstein, 1994). The terms *addictive disorder* and *addiction* are used interchangeably (Armstrong, Feigenbaum, Savage, Snow & Vourakis, 2005). Addiction is an illness that causes major impairment, but which will respond to comprehensive and varied treatment approaches which foster the patient's active participation and acceptance of responsibility.

Addiction is multidimensional, with multiple causes. One model that explains the etiology of addiction is the *biopsychosocial model* (Allen, 1996). In this explanation, addiction develops as a result of one or a combination of the following:

- Biological vulnerability (including neurochemical, genetic, and hereditary)
- Environmental vulnerability and exposure to risk factors (in utero exposure, etc.)
- Access to substances or activities (e.g. gambling)
- Predisposition to addictive behaviors and reinforcement when using/abusing
- Enabling behaviors by the individuals and systems around the person
- Environmental, cultural, or community influences, and learning processes

Addiction represents only one end of a continuum where problems associated with the use of addictive substances or behaviors are the most severe and disabling. However, there are other points on the continuum, including low risk, at risk, problem use/misuse/abuse, and dependence where intervention can occur based on the stage of change and level of motivation to change (CSAT: SAMHSA, 1997).

Process of Addiction

The U.S. Substance Abuse and Mental Health Services Administration's (SAMHSA) Center for Substance Abuse Treatment (SAMHSA, 1994) describes the five stages of the process of addiction:

1. Experimental/social use
2. Problem use/misuse/abuse
3. Dependency/addiction
4. Recovery
5. Relapse

The content in this appendix is not current and is of historical significance only.

During *recovery*, the person experiences a remission, where the addictive behavior is discontinued. Dramatic lifestyle changes occur and their effects are evident in personal and professional aspects of life. However, the chance for a relapse with the return to the previous addiction state and the person's life again being out of control remains. (SAMHSA, 1994)

During the *relapse* phase, there has been a re-occurrence of symptoms of dependence/addiction.

Diagnosing Addiction

Nurses practicing in any clinical setting will encounter patients exhibiting symptoms that point to addiction. As providers of holistic, effective, and safe care, nurses need to be aware of their role in clarifying their suspicions with an assessment and then referring patients for appropriate diagnosis and care.

One of the significant changes in the addictions field is the increased clarity in symptoms used for diagnosing problem use/substance abuse and addiction/substance dependence. *Diagnostic and Statistical Manual of Mental Disorders, 4th Edition Text Revision* (DSM-IV-TR; American Psychiatric Association, 2000) presents the criteria for diagnosing problem use/substance abuse: a maladaptive pattern of the behavior exists to the point that clinically significant impairment or distress, as manifested by one or more of the following, occurs within a 12-month period:

- Recurrent participation in the behavior results in a failure to fulfill major role obligations at work, school, or home.

- Recurrent participation in the behavior occurs in situations in which it is physically hazardous.

- Recurrent participation in the behavior leads to legal problems

- Participation in the behavior continues despite persistent social or interpersonal problems caused or exacerbated by the effects of the addictive behavior.

The diagnosis of substance dependency/addiction occurs when three or more or more of the following occur within a 12-month period:

- Tolerance: either a markedly increased intake of the substance is needed to achieve the same effect *or* with continued use, the same amount of the substance has markedly less effect.

- Withdrawal: the substance's characteristic withdrawal syndrome is experienced or the substance (or one closely related) is used to avoid or relieve withdrawal symptoms.

The content in this appendix is not current and is of historical significance only.

- The amount or duration of use is often greater than intended.

- The patient repeatedly tries without success to control or reduce substance use.

- The patient spends much time using the substance, recovering from its effects, or trying to obtain it.

- The patient reduces or abandons important work, social, or leisure activities because of substance abuse.

- The patient continues to use the substance, despite knowing that it has probably caused ongoing physical or psychological problems.

The Continuum of Care for Addictions Nursing

Prevention

Prevention is an anticipatory process that prepares and supports individuals and systems in the creation and reinforcement of healthy behaviors and lifestyles (SAMHSA, 1994). Primary prevention is the reduction or control of causative factors for addiction, and includes reducing risk factors, increasing protective factors, and participating in health service interventions (Teutsch, 1992).

- A *risk factor* is an attitude, belief, behavior, situation, or action that may put a person, group, organization, or community at risk for experiencing addiction. Risk factors should be assessed including biological and environmental vulnerability. Biological vulnerability includes genetic neurochemical predisposition. Risk factors from the environment include traumatic life events, such as sexual, physical, or emotional abuse, and chronic family stress (Snow, 2000a).

- A *protective factor* is an attitude, belief, situation, or action that protects an individual, group, organization, or community from the effects of addictions (SAMHSA, [CSAP] 1994). Protective factors provide resiliency in preventing the development of substance use disorders and other addictions, so that even if the person has numerous risk factors present, there is a buffer that helps prevents abuse or dependence from developing. Having a caring role model as a child is one of the strongest protective factors in prevention of abuse or dependence, much as effectiveness in work, play, and relationships are protective factors for adults (Snow, 2000a). Other protective factors include faith, spirituality, and religious behavior (Booth & Martin, 1998).

The content in this appendix is not current and is of historical significance only.

A variety of public policies are aimed at prevention of addictions including:

- Legal sanctions
- Decreasing availability
- Use of warning labels
- Removal of cigarette vending machines from public areas
- Prohibiting smoking in public areas
- Increasing alcohol and cigarette taxes
- Random breath testing of drivers
- Raising the legal drinking age
- Increasing sanctions for using or selling illicit drugs
- Increasing server liability
- Workforce initiatives, such as random drug testing

Combined grassroots level community, federal, and state legislative activities have resulted in funded prevention programs targeting vulnerable populations, such as youth, women, and people of color. The U.S. Substance Abuse and Mental Health Services Administration's (SAMHSA) Center for Substance Abuse Prevention (CSAP) initiatives during the 1990s focused on enhancing prevention strategies via training programs for healthcare providers, including training and development of generalist registered nurses, as well as specialty addictions nurses. The numerous CSAP-funded demonstration projects revealed "best practices" information that nurses can use to prevent addictions in their practices. (Allen, 1996; SAMHSA, 1994). Health services research is needed to measure the effectiveness and cost-effectiveness of prevention strategies, to reduce the demand for future healthcare services, and to assess how effective prevention programs are in populations that use high levels of healthcare services (National Advisory Council on Alcohol Abuse and Alcoholism, 1997). See Appendix A for a more detailed description of specific prevention strategies.

Early Intervention (Brief Interventions)

The use of *brief intervention* (BI) has become increasingly important in the continuum of care, particularly with the healthcare system now a managed care model, with reduced reimbursement policies for addiction. BI provides clinicians with intervention strategies for patients engaging in risk use that can increase positive outcomes and reduce the harmful effects of substance use (Sullivan & Fleming, 1997).

The content in this appendix is not current and is of historical significance only.

Brief interventions include advising the patient about the effects of drug or alcohol use or other at risk behaviors on health status and linking the behaviors with negative health outcomes. Strategies include reviewing findings with the patient, providing educational information (e.g. brochures, reading materials, videotapes) and counseling (Sullivan & Fleming, 1997). Assessing the patient's stage of behavioral change (i.e., pre-contemplation, contemplation, preparation, action, maintenance, and relapse) and providing interventions appropriate to the stage of change is done in a matter-of-fact, non-judgmental manner (Snow, 2000a; Dyehouse & Sommers, 1998). BI, which is timely, focused, and patient-centered, can quickly engage the patient in a therapeutic relationship that promotes behavioral change. Motivating the patient to decide to reduce or eliminate behaviors that demonstrate at risk, or mild to moderate problem use/abuse is referred to as "early intervention." See Appendix B for further discussion of motivational interventions.

Treatment

The Principles of Drug Addiction Treatment (NIDA, 1999) can apply to all addictions. The thirteen principles of *effective* treatment are:

1. No single treatment is appropriate for all persons.

2. Treatment needs to be readily available.

3. Effective treatment attends to multiple needs of the individual.

4. An individual's treatment and services plan must be assessed continually and modified as necessary to ensure that the plan meets the person's changing needs.

5. Remaining in treatment for an adequate period is critical for treatment effectiveness.

6. Counseling (individual or group) and other behavioral therapies are critical components of effective treatment for addiction.

7. Medications are an important element of treatment for many patients, especially when combined with counseling and other behavioral therapies.

8. Addicted individuals with coexisting mental disorders should have both disorders treated in an integrated way.

9. Medical detoxification is only the first stage of addiction treatment and by itself does little to change long-term drug use.

10. Treatment does not need to be voluntary to be effective.

The content in this appendix is not current and is of historical significance only.

11. Possible lapses into the addictive behavior during the time of treatment must be monitored continuously.

12. Treatment programs should provide assessment for HIV/AIDS, hepatitis B and C, tuberculosis, and other infectious diseases, as well as counseling to help patients modify behaviors that place themselves or others at risk of infection.

13. Recovery from drug addiction can be a long-term process and frequently requires multiple episodes of treatment.

Treatment for addiction and addictive behaviors can be delivered in many different settings. Patients who are participating in treatment for their addictive behaviors are usually in the dependence/addiction stage of the process of addiction. Specialized treatment facilities provide detoxification, counseling, behavioral therapy, medication therapy, case management, and other services from a comprehensive, holistic perspective. These facilities are usually part of local, state, or federal governments and provide detoxification, short-term, residential, or long-term treatment. Treatment can also occur in mental health facilities, clinics, outpatient settings, patient homes, halfway houses, and community-based facilities. Since high rates of other psychiatric disorders co-occur with addiction, many treatment facilities offer dual diagnosis or MISA (mental illness/substance abuse) programs that integrate treatment of co-occurring disorders, such as bipolar disorder, schizophrenia, major depressive disorder, and anxiety disorders with the treatment of a substance use disorder.

Some treatment approaches are specific to setting, but for the most part a variety of therapeutic services and interventions (both behavioral and pharmacological) can be provided in any given setting.

- Cognitive behavioral therapy, motivational interviewing, and brief solution therapy are treatment modalities offered in most treatment programs. Most therapies are offered in groups.

- Exercise, leisure time activities, and stress management are also important components in comprehensive treatment.

- Treatment may also include complementary therapies, such as acupuncture treatment for detoxification, relaxation and imagery, nutritional supplements and antioxidants, and yoga.

- Pharmacological management is used for detoxification, to decrease craving, to manage symptoms associated with withdrawal, for aversion behavioral therapy (e.g. disulfiram), and for treating co-occurring disorders such as bipolar disorder, major depressive disorder, panic disorder and other anxiety disorders, and schizophrenia.

The content in this appendix is not current and is of historical significance only.

Most treatment programs collaborate with self-help community programs. Self-help is not "treatment" per se, but is most often considered to be an integral aspect of recovery. Self-help groups can complement and extend the effects of professional treatment. The most prominent self-help groups are those affiliated with Alcoholics Anonymous (AA), Narcotics Anonymous (NA), Cocaine Anonymous (CA), Overeaters Anonymous (OA), Sex Anonymous (SA), Gamblers Anonymous (GA), etc. They are all based on the 12-step model. Most patients are encouraged to identify and participate in self-help programs early in intervention and treatment.

Recovery and Relapse Prevention

Persons in the recovery and relapse prevention stage of the process of addiction are often involved in a self-help program or other community support groups (e.g. AA, NA). Self-help and support programs also exist for family members and significant others of patients who are addicted (e.g. AlAnon, NarAnon, and GamAnon). Knowledge about self-help programs increases the ability of nurses to provide adequate support for patients and families with an addiction.

Recovery is enhanced by a focus on lifestyle changes, resolution of grief, family of origin issues, parenting concerns, developmental stages, self management skills, management of symptoms of mental illness such as depression and anxiety, treatment of physical illness, legal and financial stressors, and spiritual health. Ongoing care is critical to recovery and includes an interdisciplinary team to support the patient in the process of recovery.

Persons in the recovery and relapse prevention stage are at risk for relapse at any time. A full-sustained remission for drug and alcohol abuse or dependence is considered to be 12 months without having met any criteria (APA, 2000). Craving may be a strong factor that contributes to the risks for relapse for any addiction. The nurse's role is crucial, including motivating and encouraging the patient during recovery, monitoring for risk factors and symptoms, and intervening early if there is a re-occurrence of symptoms.

Description of Addictions Nursing

Addictions nursing is a distinct specialty practice that integrates biological, behavioral, environmental, psychological, social, and spiritual aspects of human responses to the illness of addiction into the nursing care provided to those affected by this disorder/disease, regardless of the clinical setting. The

The content in this appendix is not current and is of historical significance only.

scope of addictions nursing practice exists on a continuum that ranges from providing care when a problem may not exist (prevention) to providing care when addiction is present.

Addictions nursing practice is knowledge-specific, rather than setting-dependent (Vourakis, 1996), because the potential or actual responses to addictive substances or behaviors manifest themselves in a wide variety of presentations. Wherever nurses practice, they encounter people who are facing issues related to addiction, and must use their knowledge of how addiction develops, the consequences it creates, the processes for preventing the disease or relapses of the disease, and the processes for promoting individual, family, and community health. This knowledge is drawn from the biological, psychological, social, spiritual, and behavioral sciences. Addictions nurses also need a thorough understanding of pathophysiology, neurochemistry, the stages of change in relation to behavior, and the use or overuse of psychological defenses. Addictions nurses need interpersonal skills, critical thinking skills, knowledge of social systems, skill in consultation and collaboration, pharmacology skills, and therapy or counseling skills.

Addictions nurses provide direct care services, but they also consult with other providers, design programs, advocate for clients, and help to shape public policy and access to care. They may choose to specialize their practice to focus on:

- Individuals
- Families
- Communities
- Population or target groups within populations, such as women and children
- Dually diagnosed (MISA) persons with co-occurring disorders (those individuals with two or more DSM-IV diagnoses)
- The elderly
- Specific ethnic or cultural groups

Addictions nurses use knowledge of financing, systems development and change, and awareness of legal and ethical issues to formulate effective policies and procedures. They use evidence-based knowledge to continue to develop and provide state-of-the-art practice. The goal is to provide holistic care that is accessible to all.

Addictions nursing strategies or interventions may be wellness-oriented and focused on health promotion and disease prevention, or they may be illness-oriented and focused on prompt and appropriate treatment of medical

The content in this appendix is not current and is of historical significance only.

conditions associated with addiction. Interventions can also be recovery-oriented with a focus on creating the conditions that foster sobriety, serenity, relapse prevention, and reintegration into effective family, community, school, and work lives.

Phenomena of Concern

Addictions nurses in any clinical setting are concerned with patients with actual or potential responses to addictive substances and behaviors. Because those responses may exist at any point of the wellness–illness continuum, addictions nurses are concerned with:

- Conditions which increase vulnerability to or risk for addiction
- Consequences and impairment that occur when people use those substances or behaviors
- Responses of people to dependence on addictive substances or behaviors
- Conditions that affect recovery and rehabilitation

These responses can be grouped by the following categories, expanded in Table 1 on pages 17–20:

- Physiological effects
- Psychological effects
- Spiritual effects
- Cognitive effects
- Effects on family
- Social/community effects, workplace effects
- Legal effects

The content in this appendix is not current and is of historical significance only.

TABLE 1. ADDICTIONS PHENOMENA OF CONCERN

Physiological Effects:

(Note: These vary based on the substance used and its pharmacological properties)

- Altered levels of central nervous system responsiveness such as hyperactivity, seizures, and sleep disorders

- Chronic neurological conditions such as neuronal membrane changes, changes in neurochemical processes of the brain, brain cell deterioration, and peripheral nerve deterioration

- Altered psychomotor patterns such as tremors, increased or decreased sensitivity of reflexes

- Alterations of digestive system, including nausea, vomiting, anorexia, nutritional imbalances, chronic gastritis, ulceration of stomach or small intestine, pancreatitis, diarrhea, and constipation

- Alterations in immune system causing increased susceptibility to infections and problems combating infections, such as skin infections, pneumonia, and potential development of HIV infections

- Alterations in cardiovascular system, such as endocarditis, arrhythmias, peripheral vascular disease, alcoholic cardiomyopathy, and hypertension

- Chronic and disabling physical disease processes, including tissue damage, biochemical changes in major organs, and nutritional deficiencies caused by malnutrition, maldigestion, and malabsorption

- Endocrine disorders caused by changes in levels of production of hormones, such as Cushing's syndrome and impotence

- Hepatic disorders, such as fatty liver, hepatitis, and cirrhosis

- Respiratory disorders, including destruction of nasal tissues and structures, upper respiratory infections, emphysema, lung cancer, tuberculosis, and aspiration pneumonia

- Pain syndromes such as neuropathy, decreased response to pain

- Increased risk of transmission of sexually transmitted diseases such as HIV/AIDS, hepatitis C, chlamydia

- Perinatal/neonatal damage, such as fetal alcohol effects, fetal alcohol syndrome, low birth weight, irritability, neuro-developmental delays

- Sleep disorders such as insomnia, nightmares, poor sleep architecture

- Neurochemical or genetic predisposition to developing additional addictions

The content in this appendix is not current and is of historical significance only.

TABLE 1. ADDICTIONS PHENOMENA OF CONCERN

Psychological Effects:

- Depression, anxiety, shame, anger, denial, conflict within the family, remorse, alienation, fear of discovery, fear of abandonment, loss of control. Chronic tension, irritability, inability to relax without addictive substance or behavior, aggressiveness

- Increased anger and impulse control problems, resulting in family, marital, or other types of violence, physical and mental abuse, suicide ideation and attempts

- Psychiatric disorders and unmanageable feeling states, such as guilt, hopelessness, helplessness, and powerlessness

- Psychosis, paranoia, hallucinations, depersonalization

- Disruption in self-concept; deteriorating sense of self-worth; excessive use of defenses, including denial, rationalization, projection; narrowing of coping skills repertoire

- Learning disabilities, disruptive behaviors, decreased attention in children

Spiritual Effects:

- Disruption in spiritual connectedness
- Diminished purpose in life
- Feelings of meaninglessness
- Loss of control over self
- Powerlessness
- Helplessness
- Hopelessness
- Worthlessness
- Guilt

Cognitive Effects:

- Problems in acquisition of new information, problems in learning new life skills and healthy patterns of living
- Altered states of consciousness, clouded sensorium, delirium
- Impaired problem-solving abilities
- Impaired judgment
- Distorted views of the world and other people
- Disordered thought processes
- Lack of insight into the relationship between addiction and its impact

The content in this appendix is not current and is of historical significance only.

TABLE 1. ADDICTIONS PHENOMENA OF CONCERN

Effects on Family:

- Family life disruption, crises precipitated by an individual's patterns of addictive behavior
- Altered communication patterns and role performance
- Marital infidelity, nonsupport of dependents
- Enabling and rescuing behaviors, including efforts to assist the person with abuse/ dependency to escape consequences
- Multigenerational dysfunctional patterns of relating and coping that are passed on to later generations.
- Unpredictable behavior at home, financial problems
- Family processes structured around the addiction
- Isolation, lack of maturity
- Attempts to control use
- Inconsistent family structure, rigid roles and rules, closed system
- Co-dependency with poor boundaries, lack of personal control
- Children assuming roles of parents (role reversal)
- Increased use of healthcare resources
- Instability, mistrust
- Effects of addicted family member on children's emotional development
- Giving birth to children with fetal alcohol effects, fetal alcohol syndrome, and neonatal abstinence syndrome

Social/Community Effects:

- Disturbed relationships, altered productivity at work, inability to behave according to socially acceptable norms, deterioration in social life and interactions with friends, spouses, and significant others
- Interference with normal growth and development of individuals, families, and communities
- Increased criminal activity, violence
- Advertising of addictive substances concentrated in vulnerable neighborhoods
- Norms within community which condone use of addictive substances/behaviors
- Transient residents

The content in this appendix is not current and is of historical significance only.

TABLE 1. ADDICTIONS PHENOMENA OF CONCERN

- Risk factors such as poverty, racism, easy access to substances unemployment, lack of housing
- Strained existing resources, problems with access to services
- Homelessness

Workplace Effects:

- Lack of polices and prevention efforts
- Stressful environments which increase vulnerability to use addictive substances or behaviors
- Employee turnover, absenteeism, lateness
- Decreased morale
- On-the-job accidents
- Violence in the workplace
- Costs to society, including lost productivity, destruction of property and lives, excessive personnel hours required to manage problems related to addiction in the workplace
- Inconsistent behavior at work
- Deterioration in work performance

Legal Effects:

- Driving under the influence
- Prostitution
- Arrests for disturbing the peace
- Increased criminal activity
- Illegal drug sales and distribution systems
- Domestic violence and other violence charges
- Court-ordered evaluation and treatment
- Bankruptcy
- Theft, shoplifting
- Underage use

Special Diagnostic Phenomena

Addictions and addictive behaviors can be associated with other diagnostic phenomena that nurses repeatedly confront. These may include: HIV/AIDS; sexually-transmitted diseases; co-occurring primary addictions and psychiatric disorders; hepatitis; tuberculosis; domestic, family, institutional, interpersonal, and community violence; spinal cord and other disabilities; chronic conditions leading to inadequate pain management; and lung, throat, mouth, and other cancers.

Specialty Practice: Generalist Level

Addictions specialty nurses at the generalist level have expertise in prevention, interventions, and treatment for patients, their families, and groups of individuals affected by addiction. Depending on the clinical setting, they address low risk, at risk, problem use/misuse/abuse and dependency/addiction. These nurses possess demonstrated clinical skills within the specialty, exceeding those of a novice in the field, and have completed additional preparation such as enhanced educational preparation through formal classes in addiction, attendance at professional conferences, informal training through hands-on experience, distance learning through correspondence and Internet courses, and time spent in public self-help groups not related to their own support or recovery.

The nurse's expertise is based on the knowledge and clinical skills required to address alterations in all dimensions of the human system (psychological, biological, cognitive, social, and spiritual) affected by addiction. Such skills include counseling, health education, screening and assessment, clinical interventions aimed at reducing the consequences of addiction, and the promotion of self-management.

Generalist level addictions nursing practice is characterized by interventions that promote and foster health, assess abuse/dependency, assist patients and families to regain or improve their coping mechanisms, and prevent relapse. The nurse should be skilled in developing a therapeutic relationship with patients to foster collaboration in implementation of the plan of care. The patient may be an individual, a family or network of significant others, a group of individuals, or a community.

Addictions Nursing: Scope and Standards of Practice

The content in this appendix is not current and is of historical significance only.

The following skills and knowledge are foundational for the practice of addictions nursing at the generalist level:

- Theoretical and clinical knowledge at the generalist level of nursing education

- Knowledge and skills in comprehensive nursing assessment, including interviewing, taking a health history, conducting a physical examination, psychosocial assessment, mental status examination, family assessment, and community assessment

- Knowledge and skills related to the use of screening and assessment tools with specific addictive disorders

- Self-awareness as a basis for enhancing engagement with the patient in a therapeutic relationship

- Knowledge of patterns of addiction and the behavioral and physiological responses that accompany these patterns

- Counseling skills with individuals, groups, and families including:
  a) Formal and informal approaches
  b) Techniques specific to substance use and other addictive disorders
  c) Counseling goals:
     1) Development of therapeutic relationship or alliance
     2) Understanding of the health consequences and risks
     3) Identification of unhealthy coping mechanisms
     4) Motivational interviewing to modify the client's view of self and the world
     5) Identifying stage of change and readiness for change
     6) Promoting healthy constructive thoughts, behaviors, and coping strategies
     7) Positive reinforcement for modification of the patient's family, work, and living environments

When working in a residential, community, or hospital-based setting, the addictions nurse has a pivotal role in the development and maintenance of a therapeutic milieu within the treatment unit or program. The goal is to develop mutual respect with the patient in order to provide guidance, support, and direction as the recovery process begins.

The content in this appendix is not current and is of historical significance only.

Evaluation of the treatment plan and progress in its implementation are continuous and systematic. Because addictions are illnesses characterized by periods of progress and relapse, progress, or lack of progress, toward identified goals requires periodic assessment of the patient's status. This allows the nurse to assist the patient or family in the reformulation of goals, interventions, or a change in priorities. The patient's participation in setting goals and in implementing the treatment plan is an important part of recovery.

Specialty Practice: Advanced Level

The advanced practice registered nurse in addictions (APRN-A) manages patients with addictions and related health problems using a high level of expertise in the assessment, diagnosis, and management of the complex responses of individuals, families, or communities. As well, the APRN-A plans prevention programs in communities through advocacy and planning skills, and influences health policy. Accordingly, the APRN-A has a master's or doctoral degree with a strong focus in addictions, including co-occurring problems of a psychiatric or medical nature or public health and community focus. In addition, during graduate education the APRN-A has clinical experiences focused on addictions practice and continues ongoing clinical experiences related to addictions following graduation.

In addition to the basic addictions nursing practice skills and knowledge, the APRN in addictions has the preparation and skills, based on their educational experience and practice to:

- Complete comprehensive health assessment including complete history, physical examination when appropriate, and mental status assessment.
- Formulate clinical decisions to manage acute and chronic addictions-related illness.
- Provide direct care that includes screening, assessment, diagnosis, and development of a comprehensive treatment plan.
- Order laboratory and other tests.
- Prescribe medications for: management of intoxication, overdose, withdrawal, craving; substitution therapy; and symptom management for co-occurring psychiatric disorders (for APRN-As with prescriptive authority and educational preparation).
- Prescribe nonpharmacological treatments related to addictions and associated health problems.
- Conduct psychotherapy including individual, couples, group, or family.

The content in this appendix is not current and is of historical significance only.

- Implement health promotion and disease prevention interventions related to addictions.

- Include relevant teaching plans.

- Make accurate referrals and consultations.

- Evaluate outcomes of interventions.

- Conduct or actively participate in addictions research.

- Serve as leader and mentor.

- Collaborate and function as an integral member of an interdisciplinary team.

Some APRN-As have completed a Clinical Nurse Specialist-focused master's degree program or a primary care or specialty (e.g., Psychiatric Mental Health Nurse Practitioner) master's degree Nurse Practitioner program. Other advanced degrees prepare the addictions nurse to focus more on community assessment, population focused interventions, and research aimed at improving the health of communities.

The APRN in addictions combines case management functions with population-specific nursing knowledge, research competencies, expertise in psychotherapy, and the ability to work with complex and severe addictions problems. In community and primary settings, the APRN in addictions, in a leadership role, analyzes the health needs of both individuals and populations, and designs programs that target at-risk groups and cultural and environmental factors, foster health, and prevent abuse and addiction.

The APRN in addictions frequently provides clinical supervision to assist others to further develop their clinical skills. Consultation to healthcare providers and others regarding quality of care related to addictions issues, e.g. detoxification protocols in a general medical setting, can be a significant part of the role.

Additional Activities of Addictions Nurses

Addictions nursing encompasses both prevention of health problems and promotion of optimal health for the individual and society through education. Nurses, as recognized authorities on health, can educate individuals, groups, and communities about risk and protective factors, as well as characteristics of addictive substances. Nurses may integrate experiential learning opportunities to help the learner develop understanding of abuse and addictions and the skills to learn to cope with them.

Health teaching includes communicating about healthy behaviors and relationships, harm reduction strategies, as well as dysfunctional interpersonal and familial patterns, such as codependency and dysfunctional parenting. The nurse works with patients in their activities of daily living to promote adherence to an appropriate health regimen aimed at abstinence from mood altering chemicals, interruption in the compulsive behavior patterns, and effective interaction patterns with significant others.

Case management is a clinical component of the addictions nurse's role in both inpatient and outpatient settings. Nurse case managers employ culturally relevant interventions designed to support the patient's highest level of functioning, enhanced recovery, and progress toward optimal health. The case manager identifies and coordinates various other health and human services as resources for care.

A particularly important role of the addictions nurse is that of advocate, for the purpose of influencing policy. The nursing profession supports each person's right to health care, regardless of social or economic status, personal attributes, or the nature of the person's health problems. Addictions nurses have long fought the battle to help society understand the disease concept of addiction and recognize that addictions treatment works. Their work in state and federal organizations has resulted in increased funding for treatment agencies and research.

Addictions nurses are joining professional or consumer groups to abolish the stigma attached to addictions and to achieve parity between addictions, mental health, and physical illness insurance benefits. These nurses not only support legislation and community action, but also use their professional and political skills to promote the expansion of the healthcare system to address problems of abuse and addiction (e.g. issues of access to care).

In clinical practice, the addictions nurse advocates for the rights of patients. Because of a strong commitment to the health, welfare, and safety of the patient, nurses must be aware of any activity which places the rights or well-being of the patient in jeopardy and take appropriate action on the patient's behalf. It is imperative that addictions nurses working in the community in a variety of settings (public health, free clinic, homeless shelter, methadone clinic) be aware of all the community resources available to the patient and assist the patient in accessing these services. Involvement with community planning boards, advisory groups, paraprofessionals and other key people is an important means by which nurses can mobilize the community's resources and bring about changes that address abuse and addictions needs of particular population groups (adolescents, women, elderly, etc.). See Appendix C for the Code of Ethics for Addictions Nurses, which guides addictions nurses in their practice.

The content in this appendix is not current and is of historical significance only.

Education for Addictions Nursing Practice

Educational preparation for addictions nursing practice has lagged behind education for other nursing specialties. Federal initiatives have attempted to address this lack of attention to one of the nation's major health problems. The National Institute on Alcohol Abuse and Alcoholism (NIAAA), the National Institute on Drug Abuse (NIDA), and the Office for Substance Abuse Prevention (now the Center for Substance Abuse Prevention) have supported curriculum and faculty development in schools of nursing over the past two decades. As a result of these curriculum grants, several model curricula designed to incorporate addiction information into nursing education at the undergraduate and graduate levels are available for use in undergraduate and graduate nursing programs (Burns, Thompson & Ciccone, 1991; McRee, Babor & Church, 1991; Naegle & D'Arcangelo, 1991).

The generally held public belief that addiction is a moral issue associated with poor judgment, poor impulse control, bad behavior, and an unwillingness to quit using has been the beliefs of some nurses. Research findings support the need for inclusion of addictions content in both undergraduate and graduate nursing curricula. A possible reason for nurses' negative attitudes and false beliefs about addictions has been the lack of evidence-based content about addictions in the nursing curriculum (Starkey, 1980; Smith, 1992; Happell & Taylor, 1999). Inclusion of essential content based on current research and best practices will result in nursing students acquiring the basic skills related to the care of persons with addictions and remove the stigma often associated with addictions (Reisman and Schrader, 1984; Tamlyn 1989; Martinez and Murphy-Parker, 2003). This will in turn affect the quality of care a nurse gives to the addicted client. Several models of curriculum content in addictions have been suggested.

Presently in nursing education much of the emphasis on addictions is related to patients who are currently experiencing addiction and in treatment. Suggested models for curriculum content in addictions include adding a focus on prevention and early intervention strategies, to help nursing students learn the importance of their role in helping prevent substance use disorders and other addictions. Additional suggested content in addictions includes teaching students the neuroanatomy and neurochemistry associated with addiction (Snow, 2000b), assessment for the early signs of at-risk use, brief intervention skills, assessment of withdrawal symptoms, and harm reduction principles. Additional coursework in the pharmacology of addictive substances, the process of addiction, the seductive capabilities of abused substances, and the components of a healthy lifestyle has been suggested. (National Nurses Society on Addictions, 1993)

The content in this appendix is not current and is of historical significance only.

Other models of curriculum in nursing education related to addictions have been suggested. Recommended content includes the etiology of abuse and dependence, the consequences associated with abuse, the care of affected family members and others surrounding the person relying on addictive substances or behaviors, methods for mobilizing community efforts, treatment and self-help, and the prevention of addiction among healthcare professionals. Addictions content ideally should be integrated throughout nursing curricula, since issues related to addiction occur at all stages of health and disease. It is also recommended that schools of nursing consider development of a policy which offers support for nursing students when they themselves, or a close family member or friend, are experiencing problems with addictions (Murphy-Parker, Knonenbitter & Knonenbitter, 2003; NNSA, 1993; Sullivan, 1995) In addition, undergraduate students need clinical experiences with clients who have addictions-related problems.

Graduate education for specialty practice in addictions nursing should include comprehensive theoretical and research-based content on addictions and development of clinical skills, including screening, comprehensive assessment, differential diagnosis, interventions directed at individuals, families, and communities, and strategies for prevention and rehabilitation. Their clinical practice will include assessment and intervention in various environments that are culture-specific, such as homeless shelters and community centers, as well as office practices, outpatient and hospital settings, home care, and outpatient detoxification. Advanced practice nurses working in other specialty areas should be adequately prepared to screen and assess patients with addictions and refer them to specialty care as needed.

In addition to providing model curricula, federal grants have prepared a cadre of faculty with expertise in alcohol and other drug-related disorders. These faculty serve as resources in their schools, assist in incorporating and implementing addictions content into the curriculum, teach addictions nursing courses, and publish articles about their activities, contributing to the body of knowledge about current and future addictions nursing practice (Gerace, Sullivan, Murphy & Cotter, 1992; Hagemaster, Plumlee, Connors, & Sullivan, 1994; Marcus, Gerace & Sullivan, 1996; 1996, Marcus, 1997).

Certification

A nurse who has the designation of "addictions nurse" meets the specialty's standards of knowledge and experience through certification as a Certified Addictions Registered Nurse (CARN). The CARN has met the qualifications in experience, education, and testing to be recognized in the specialty of

The content in this appendix is not current and is of historical significance only.

addictions nursing at the generalist level. This certification has been offered by the Addictions Nursing Certification Board of the International Nurses Society on Addictions since 1989.

The advanced practice certification for addictions nurses (Certified Addictions Registered Nurse-Advanced Practice, CARN-AP) was first offered by the Addictions Nursing Certification Board of the International Nurses Society on Addictions in 2000. It is based on a national job analysis of the role of the advanced practice nurse in addictions. Criteria for achieving this certification include a master's degree with a specified number of documented hours in advanced practice addictions nursing and a passing score on the certification exam.

Certified Addictions Registered Nurses—CARN and CARN-AP—care for individuals across the life span, their families, and with entire populations. These certified nurses have the potential to reduce the harm to individuals and society related to the use of alcohol, tobacco, and other drugs, and other addictions such as gambling (Finnell, 2002).

Implications for Research

Scientific advances in the specialty of addictions have proliferated in the past few years. Current neurobiological researchers have focused on how addictive substances affect the central nervous system, including the role of neurotransmitters and receptor sites for opiates, alcohol, benzodiazepines, and other substances. Researchers concerned with treatment outcomes have provided evidence to support best practices in relation to treatment for addictions based on specific patient characteristics. Genetic researchers are identifying specific genes involved in addiction, and family pedigree studies hold promise for prevention and early treatment. Transcultural researchers have provided insight into addictions related to specific groups and populations.

Nursing research in addictions is currently contributing to knowledge related to the etiology, prevention, and treatment of addiction. Federally funded faculty development grants have helped ameliorate this deficit, but scientific evidence on the nursing care of persons with addiction disorders needs further research. Recent funding of nurse scientists to conduct alcohol and other drug research through the National Institute on Alcohol Abuse and Alcoholism and the National Institute on Drug Abuse at the National Institutes of Health will help build the nursing science in addictions. Research in addictions nursing is crucial in leading the search for scientifically tested, appropriate, and effective interventions (Compton, 1996). In particular, nurse

The content in this appendix is not current and is of historical significance only.

researchers are needed who will provide the evidence to support nursing interventions aimed at prevention and treatment of addictive disorders related to individuals, families, groups, and communities.

In addition, more research is needed in relation to other forms of addiction, including those classified as addictive behaviors. Nurse scientists are needed who will study all aspects of such addictions as gambling, eating disorders, and sexual addictions. Finally, nurses must disseminate their research findings and build new evidence-based models of treatment. *Journal of Addictions Nursing* provides a vehicle for addictions nurse researchers as well as other addictions researchers to communicate their findings. To meet this objective, additional nurse scientists interested in addictions nursing are needed in doctoral programs. This will increase the total number of addictions nurse researchers available as principal investigators, project directors, educators, and authors of research-based journal articles. Multiple sources of financial support for doctoral education and for research studies must be identified in order for this strategy to be successful.

Nurses must use research-validated and scientific approaches to addictions prevention and treatment. All nurses, including addictions nurses, need to understand evidence-based practice and make that concept a routine part of professional practice.

Peer Assistance

Nurses are vulnerable to the disease of addiction as are other healthcare professionals. Trinkoff, Eaton & Anthony (1991) reported that 17% of nurses reported heavy alcohol use and 3.8% reported illicit drug use. The nurse's license is subject to revocation if there are impaired practice violations related to addictions or other serious psychiatric disorders. Also, patients may suffer harm from the nurse's impaired behavior. Yet nurses with dependence/addiction, like other persons with dependence/addiction, continue to abuse drugs and alcohol despite the risk of major consequences. Interventions are often done by peers to encourage and motivate the nurse to seek help. Nurses have an ethical obligation to advocate for their colleagues who manifest impaired practice and motivate them to seek help through their state peer assistance program, if available. If there is not a peer assistance program then the nurse must be referred to the State Board of Nursing and disciplinary action may ensue.

Peer assistance programs that are alternative to discipline programs are offered in most states to provide monitoring, counseling and case management so that the nurse who is willing to seek help and recovery from

The content in this appendix is not current and is of historical significance only.

the addiction or mental disorder does not face disciplinary action with the State Board of Nursing. Nurses continue in the program in most states for two years, during which time they return to work with some restrictions on their practice (e.g. not being able to work extra shifts).

Nursing organizations, such as the International Nurses Society on Addictions, advocate for all nurses who need help for addictions or other psychiatric disorders to have the opportunity to participate in alternatives to discipline programs, and assist them in establishing return-to-work agreements. A national effort is underway to ensure that all states offer such programs. In 2002 the American Nurses Association passed an update of the 1980 ground-breaking resolution calling for all states to create non-disciplinary programs. The National Student Nurses Association (NSNA) also passed a resolution in 2002 calling for all schools of nursing to implement policies to support nursing students with addictions (Murphy-Parker, Kronenbitter & Kronenbitter, 2003).

The content in this appendix is not current and is of historical significance only.

STANDARDS OF CARE FOR ADDICTIONS NURSING

STANDARD 1. ASSESSMENT

The addictions nurse collects patient health data.

Measurement Criteria

1. The addictions nurse determines the priority of data collection according to the patient's immediate health needs.

2. Assessment is individualized based on the patient's age, culture, and medical and biopsychosocial needs.

3. The data are collected in a systematic and ongoing manner, including the following:

Subjective data:

- Chief complaint, symptoms, or focus of concern
- Physical, developmental, cognitive, mental, and emotional health status
- Current and past medications, including prescribed, over the counter, herbal
- Past medical, psychiatric, and addictions history
- Family history including addictions, psychiatric disorders, other health concerns
- Family, community, culture, race, ethnicity systems
- Spiritual health
- Personal, developmental, abuse, and social history
- Work or school adjustment
- Interpersonal relationships, communication skills, and coping patterns
- Current use of psychoactive substances and compulsive behaviors

Objective data:

- Physical health measurements
- Screening, diagnostic and lab measurements
- Mental status examination
- Safety, health promotion and functional assessment
- Strengths and assets that can be used to promote health

The content in this appendix is not current and is of historical significance only.

4.   Assessment is done collaboratively with interdisciplinary team members.

5.   Assessment actively includes the patient, family, other healthcare workers, social network, and past and current medical records when appropriate.

6.   Data records are synthesized, prioritized, and documented in retrievable form.

7.   Assessment techniques are based on clinical judgment and addictions research.

8.   Patient data are collected using reliable and valid addictions-specific instruments.

The content in this appendix is not current and is of historical significance only.

STANDARD 2. DIAGNOSIS

The addictions nurse analyzes the assessment data in determining diagnoses.

Measurement Criteria

1. Diagnoses and potential problem statements are derived from assessment data.

2. Interpersonal, systemic, or environmental circumstances that affect the well-being of the individual, family, or community are identified.

3. The diagnoses are based on an accepted framework that supports the addictions nursing knowledge and judgment used in analyzing the data.

4. Diagnoses are consistent with accepted classifications systems, such as North American Nursing Diagnosis Association (NANDA) *Nursing Diagnosis Classification, International Classification of Diseases* (WHO 1993), and *The Diagnostic and Statistical Manual of Mental Disorders IV-TR* (APA 2001) used in the practice setting.

5. Diagnoses and risk factors are validated with the patient, significant others, family members or guardians, and other healthcare providers when appropriate and possible.

6. Diagnoses identify actual or potential responses to addictive substances/behaviors and health problems of the patient pertaining to:

   • Maintenance of optimal health and well-being and the prevention of illness.

   • Self-care limitations or impaired functioning related to psychological and emotional distress.

   • Deficits in the functioning of significant biological, psychological, spiritual, and cognitive systems.

   • Emotional stress or crisis components of illness, pain, and disability.

   • Self-concept changes, developmental issues, and life process changes.

   • Problems related to emotions such as anxiety, aggression, sadness, loneliness, and grief.

   • Physical symptoms that occur along with altered psychological functioning.

   • Alterations in thinking, perceiving, symbolizing, communicating, and decision-making.

The content in this appendix is not current and is of historical significance only.

- Difficulties in relating to others.

- Behaviors and mental status that indicate the patient is a danger to self or others or has a severe disability.

- Interpersonal, systemic, sociocultural, spiritual, or environmental circumstances or events, which have an effect on the psychological and emotional well-being of the individual, family, or community.

- Symptom management, side effects or toxicity associated with detoxification, psychopharmacologic intervention, and other aspects of the treatment regimen.

- Symptom management related to medical illness.

7. Diagnoses and clinical impressions are documented in a manner that facilitates the identification of patient outcomes and their use in the plan of care.

The content in this appendix is not current and is of historical significance only.

STANDARD 3. OUTCOME IDENTIFICATION

The addictions nurse identifies expected outcomes individualized to the patient.

Measurement Criteria

Expected outcomes:

1. Are derived from the diagnoses.

2. Are patient-oriented, evidence-based, therapeutically sound, realistic, attainable, and cost effective.

3. Are documented as measurable goals.

4. Are formulated by the nurse and the patient, significant others, and interdisciplinary team members, when possible.

5. Are age-related, culturally appropriate and sensitive, and gender-specific, as well as realistic in relation to the patient's present and potential capabilities and quality of life.

6. Reflect considerations of the associated benefits and costs.

7. Estimate a time for attainment.

8. Provide direction for continuity of care.

9. Serve as a record of change in the patient's health status.

10. Reflect consideration of the patient's bio-psycho-socio-spiritual and cultural needs.

11. Are attainable in relation to resources available to the patient.

12. Are used in comparative data and benchmarking reports with like programs and facilities.

13. Are modified based on changes in the patient's health status.

14. Reflect current scientific knowledge in addictions care.

The content in this appendix is not current and is of historical significance only.

STANDARD 4. PLANNING

The addictions nurse develops an individualized plan of care that prescribes interventions to attain expected outcomes.

Measurement Criteria

The plan of care:

1. Is developed through collaborative efforts of the addictions nurse, the interdisciplinary treatment team, the patient, and significant others.

2. Uses the nursing process in developing and revising the plan of care.

3. Identifies priorities of care in relation to expected outcomes.

4. States realistic goals in behavioral or measurable terms with expected dates of accomplishment.

5. Incorporates psychotherapeutic and neurobiological theories and principles.

6. Specifies evidence-based interventions that reflect current best practices in addictions nursing.

7. Specifies appropriate interventions, individualized according to the patient's age, gender, developmental stage, ethnicity, and sexual orientation.

8. Includes an educational plan related to the patient's health problems, treatment plan, relapse prevention, self-care, and quality of life issues.

9. Provides the appropriate consultation, referral, and case management to ensure continuity of care.

10. Includes a plan for ongoing treatment of healthcare needs.

11. Is documented in a format that allows modification, interdisciplinary access, and retrieval of data for analysis and research when appropriate.

12. Includes strategies for health promotion, disease prevention, and restoration of health.

13. Reflects current best practices in addictions nursing practice (prevention, intervention, treatment, relapse prevention).

The content in this appendix is not current and is of historical significance only.

STANDARD 5. IMPLEMENTATION

The addictions nurse implements the interventions identified in the plan of care.

Measurement Criteria

Interventions are:

1. Implemented within the established plan of care and address identified actual or potential needs of the patient.

2. Implemented in a safe, timely, ethical, and appropriate manner.

3. Documented in a format that is related to patient outcomes, accessible to the interdisciplinary team, and retrievable.

4. Based on current scientific and theoretical knowledge.

5. Performed according to the nurse's level of education and practice.

STANDARD 5A. THERAPEUTIC ALLIANCE

The addictions nurse uses the "therapeutic self" to establish a therapeutic alliance with the patient and to structure nursing interventions to promote development of insight, coping skills, and motivation for change in behavior that promotes health.

Measurement Criteria

1. The nurse documents the presence or absence of behavior change that reflect increased knowledge and motivation for change regarding patterns of use, abuse, and dependence related to addictive substances or behaviors.

2. The nurse documents the degree to which relational skills and health promotion behaviors have been incorporated into the patient's lifestyle.

3. The relationship established between nurse and patient remains within professional and ethical boundaries.

The content in this appendix is not current and is of historical significance only.

STANDARD 5B. HEALTH TEACHING

The addictions nurse, through health teaching, assists individuals, families, groups, and communities in achieving satisfying, productive, and healthy patterns of living.

Measurement Criteria

1. Health teaching occurs in the individual, family, group, and community contexts and includes:

    *   Health promotion.
    *   Risk and protective factors
    *   Methods for strengthening resiliency
    *   Patterns of problem use, abuse and addiction
    *   Spiritual, biological, psychosocial, and cognitive components of addiction, and their impact on self, family, and community.
    *   Treatments and their effects on daily living
    *   The process of recovery and relapse prevention
    *   Physical health
    *   Social skills
    *   Developmental, gender, and cultural needs
    *   Parenting and strengthening family coping

2. Educational activities and the learning responses of the individual, family, group, and community are documented.

3. Health teaching methods and strategies are appropriate to the developmental level, learning needs, readiness and ability to learn, health status, education, and culture of the individual, family, group, and community.

The content in this appendix is not current and is of historical significance only.

STANDARD 5C. SELF-CARE AND SELF-MANAGEMENT

The addictions nurse uses the knowledge and philosophy of self-care and self-management to assist the patient in learning new ways to address stress, maintain self-control, accept personal responsibility, and integrate healthy coping behaviors into life-style choices.

Measurement Criteria

1. The self-care and self-management activities chosen are appropriate to the patient's physical and mental status as well as age, developmental level, gender, ethnicity, and education.

2. The self-care and self-management interventions assist the patient in accepting responsibility for health, including accessing available community support systems such as self-help groups, making personal lifestyle changes, setting realistic goals for behavioral change, and monitoring progress.

3. The self-care and self-management interventions extend to the family and significant others when appropriate to facilitate system change, including accessing community support systems.

4. The nurse documents the level of the patient's ability to respond to involvement in self-help or other support groups as appropriate.

The content in this appendix is not current and is of historical significance only.

STANDARD 5D. PHARMACOLOGICAL, BIOLOGICAL, AND COMPLEMENTARY THERAPIES

The addictions nurse applies knowledge of pharmacological, biological, and complementary therapies and uses clinical skills to restore the patient's health and prevent consequences from addiction.

Measurement Criteria

The addictions nurse:

1. Uses current research findings and best practices to guide nursing actions related to pharmacology, other biological therapies, and complementary therapies.

2. Monitors pharmacological agents' intended actions, untoward or interactive effects, and therapeutic doses as well as blood levels, vital signs, and laboratory values where appropriate.

3. Directs nursing interventions towards alleviating untoward effects of pharmacological, biological, and complementary therapies.

4. Uses knowledge of signs and symptoms of substance overdose, withdrawal syndrome, and multiple drug-use patterns to promote safety in treatment.

5. Uses knowledge of the appropriate pharmacological and other biological treatments of psychiatric and medical problems that commonly coexist with addictions in monitoring the patient's care.

6. Educates the patient and family of the potential for abuse of selected pharmacological agents.

7. Evaluates the patient's response to the administered medications and therapies and documents the response.

8. Communicates observations about the patient's response to pharmacological, biological, and complementary interventions to other healthcare providers when appropriate.

9. Teaches the patient the beneficial effects and potential adverse effects of prescribed medications, biological treatment, and complementary therapies.

10. Provides the patient information regarding costs of using pharmacological, biological, and complementary therapies in making informed choices.

The content in this appendix is not current and is of historical significance only.

STANDARD 5E. THERAPEUTIC MILIEU

The addictions nurse structures, provides, and maintains a therapeutic environment in collaboration with the patient and other healthcare providers.

Measurement Criteria

1. The patient is familiarized with the physical environment, the schedule of groups and activities, rights and responsibilities, the rules and regulations that govern behavior, and the goals of the treatment team.

2. Current knowledge and best practices of the effects of environment on the patient are used to promote a safe, therapeutic environment.

3. The therapeutic environment is designed in accordance with accreditation standards, utilizing the physical environment, social structure, culture, and other available resources.

4. Therapeutic communication among patients and staff supports an effective milieu.

5. Specific activities are selected that meet the patient's physical, spiritual, psychological, and behavioral health needs.

6. Limits of any kind (e.g., restriction of privileges) are the least restrictive necessary, maintain the dignity of the patient, and are used only to ensure the safety of the patient and others.

7. The patient is given information about the need for limits and the conditions necessary for removal of the restriction, as appropriate.

8. Patient orientation to, participation in, and response to the therapeutic milieu are documented.

The content in this appendix is not current and is of historical significance only.

STANDARD 5F. COUNSELING

The addictions nurse uses counseling interventions to assist patients in promoting healthy coping abilities, preventing addiction, and addressing issues related to patterns of abuse and addiction.

Measurement Criteria

1. Counseling interventions include interdisciplinary and peer collaboration to plan and facilitate achievement of counseling goals.

2. The patient is included in the planning, goal setting, and evaluation of outcomes.

3. Counseling interventions are documented on the treatment plan and medical record.

4. Confidentiality issues are managed with ethical integrity and according to federal, state, and professional confidentiality guidelines.

5. Referral sources for additional therapy, psycho-education programs (e.g. parenting classes), and self-help groups are provided to the patient and family as appropriate.

6. Counseling strategies are used to engage the patient, family, and significant others in the therapeutic process to promote improved relationships and behavioral change.

7. The addictions nurse participates in individual and group counseling within parameters of certification, state, and employer expectations

The content in this appendix is not current and is of historical significance only.

STANDARD 6. EVALUATION

The addictions nurse evaluates the patient's progress toward attainment of expected outcomes.

Measurement Criteria

1. Evaluation is systematic, ongoing, and outcome-based.

2. The patient, significant others, and healthcare providers are involved in the evaluation process, when appropriate.

3. The patient's responses to interventions are documented in a format related to expected outcomes and easily accessible to the interdisciplinary team.

4. Ongoing assessment data are used to revise diagnoses, outcomes, and the plan of care as needed.

The content in this appendix is not current and is of historical significance only.

STANDARDS OF PROFESSIONAL PERFORMANCE

STANDARD 7. QUALITY OF CARE

The addictions nurse systematically evaluates the quality of care and effectiveness of nursing practice.

Measurement Criteria

The addictions nurse:

1. Participates in outcomes-based quality improvement activities as appropriate to the nurse's position, education, and practice environment. Such activities may include:

    - Identification of aspects of care important for quality monitoring (e.g., Functional status, symptom management, safety, patient satisfaction, and quality of life)

    - Analysis of quality of care data to identify opportunities for improving care

    - Development of policies, procedures, and practice guidelines to improve quality of care

    - Identification of indicators used to monitor quality of care and effectiveness of nursing care

    - Collection of data to monitor quality of care and effectiveness of nursing care

    - Formulation of recommendations to improve nursing practice or patient outcomes

    - Implementation of activities to enhance the quality of nursing practice

    - Participation on interdisciplinary teams that evaluate clinical practice or health services

2. Uses the results of outcomes-based quality improvement activities to initiate changes in addictions nursing practice.

3. Uses the results of outcomes-based quality improvement activities to initiate changes throughout the healthcare delivery system, as appropriate.

The content in this appendix is not current and is of historical significance only.

STANDARD 8. PERFORMANCE APPRAISAL

The addictions nurse evaluates their own nursing practice in relation to professional practice standards and relevant statutes and regulations.

Measurement Criteria

The addictions nurse:

1. Engages in performance appraisal of their own clinical practice and role performance with peers or supervisors on a regular basis, identifying areas of strength as well as areas for professional and practice development.

2. Seeks constructive feedback regarding practice and role performance from peers, professional colleagues, patients, and others.

3. Takes action to achieve goals identified during performance appraisal and peer review, resulting in changes in practice and role performance.

4. Engages in a performance improvement plan seeking to achieve identified performance improvement measures related to job performance.

5. Participates in peer review activities as appropriate.

6. Self-evaluates practice based on patient outcomes and current research findings.

7. Changes practice based on knowledge of current professional practice standards, laws, and regulations.

The content in this appendix is not current and is of historical significance only.

STANDARD 9. EDUCATION

The addictions nurse acquires and maintains current knowledge and competency in nursing practice.

Measurement Criteria

The addictions nurse:

1. Participates in ongoing professional educational activities to improve clinical knowledge, enhance role performance, and increase knowledge of professional issues.

2. Seeks experience and independent learning activities that reflect current research-based clinical practice, in order to maintain and further develop clinical skills and competency.

3. Seeks additional knowledge and skills appropriate to the specialty area and practice setting by participating in educational programs and activities, conferences, workshops, and interdisciplinary professional meetings.

4. Documents their educational activities.

5. Achieves and maintains professional certification.

6. Bases practice in current scientific and theoretical knowledge and research findings.

The content in this appendix is not current and is of historical significance only.

STANDARD 10. COLLEGIALITY

The addictions nurse interacts with and contributes to the professional development of peers, and treats other healthcare providers as colleagues.

Measurement Criteria

The addictions nurse:

1. Uses opportunities in practice to exchange knowledge, skills, and clinical observations with colleagues and others.

2. Assists others in identifying teaching or learning needs related to clinical cases, role performance, and professional development.

3. Provides peers with constructive feedback regarding their practice.

4. Contributes to an environment that is conducive to the clinical education of nursing students, other healthcare students, and employees as appropriate.

5. Actively promotes interdisciplinary collaboration to enhance professional practice.

6. Contributes to a supportive and healthy work environment.

7. Participates in local, state, national, and international professional associations to address addiction.

The content in this appendix is not current and is of historical significance only.

STANDARD 11. ETHICS

The nurse's decisions and actions on behalf of patients are determined and implemented in an ethical manner.

Measurement Criteria

The addictions nurse:

1. Observes and maintains patient confidentiality within legal and regulatory parameters.

2. Uses *Code of Ethics for Nurses With Interpretive Statements* (ANA, 2001) and *Code of Ethics for Addictions Nurses* (NNSA, 1996) to guide practice.

3. Follows the ethical responsibilities and principles of conduct prescribed by the facility where they are employed.

4. Informs the patient of the risks, benefits, and expected outcomes of healthcare regimens.

5. Delivers care in a nonjudgmental and nondiscriminatory manner that is sensitive to patient diversity.

6. Delivers care in a manner that preserves patient autonomy, dignity, and rights.

7. Seeks available resources when necessary in formulating ethical decisions.

8. Contributes to resolving the ethical dilemmas or problems of patients and healthcare systems.

9. Acts as a patient advocate and assists patients in developing skills so they can advocate for themselves.

10. Performs interventions in a safe, ethical manner.

The content in this appendix is not current and is of historical significance only.

STANDARD 12. COLLABORATION

The nurse collaborates with the patient, significant others, and other healthcare providers in providing patient care.

Measurement Criteria

The addictions nurse:

1. Communicates with the patient, significant others, and other healthcare providers regarding patient care.

2. Consults with other healthcare providers regarding patient care as needed.

3. Makes referrals, including provisions for continuity of care, as needed.

4. Collaborates with the patient, family, and other healthcare providers in the formulation of outcomes of care, and in the decisions related to care and the delivery of services.

5. Collaborates with healthcare providers and members of the community to increase the community's capacity to prevent and address addictions.

The content in this appendix is not current and is of historical significance only.

STANDARD 13. RESEARCH

The addictions nurse uses theory and evidence from research findings to guide practice.

Measurement Criteria

The addictions nurse:

1. Uses interventions substantiated by theory and research, and appropriate to the nurse's position, education, and practice environment, to develop a plan of care.

2. Participates in research activities appropriate to the nurse's position, education, and practice environment. Such activities may include:

    *   Identification of clinical or behavioral health problems suitable for nursing research

    *   Participation in data collection in research projects

    *   Participation in a unit, department, organization, or community research committees or programs

    *   Sharing of research activities with others

    *   Implementation of research projects in the appropriate setting

    *   Critiquing or evaluating research for application to practice

    *   Use of research findings in the development of policies, procedures, guidelines, and benchmarks for patient care

3. Disseminates relevant research finding with nurses and other health professionals through presentations, publications, and practice.

The content in this appendix is not current and is of historical significance only.

STANDARD 14. RESOURCE UTILIZATION

The addictions nurse considers factors related to safety, effectiveness, and cost in planning and delivering patient care.

Measurement Criteria

The addictions nurse:

1. Analyzes factors related to safety, effectiveness, availability, and cost when choosing between practice options that would result in the same expected patient outcome.

2. Assists the patient and significant others in becoming informed consumers about the cost, risks, and benefits of treatment and care.

3. Assists the patient and significant others in identifying and securing appropriate and available services to address health-related needs.

4. Assigns or delegates tasks, as defined by the State Nurse Practice Acts, based on the needs and condition of the patient, and according to the knowledge and skills of the designated caregiver.

5. Participates in ongoing resource utilization review, including facility resources, marketing, and level of treatment needed by each patient.

The content in this appendix is not current and is of historical significance only.

ADVANCED PRACTICE STANDARDS OF CARE FOR ADDICTIONS NURSING

STANDARD 1. ASSESSMENT

The advanced practice addictions registered nurse collects comprehensive patient health data.

Measurement Criteria

The advanced practice addictions registered nurse:

1. Bases assessment techniques on theory, research, and best practices.

2. Initiates and interprets diagnostic tests and procedures relevant to the patient's current status as indicated.

STANDARD 2. DIAGNOSIS

The advanced practice addictions registered nurse critically analyzes the assessment data in determining the diagnoses.

Measurement Criteria

The advanced practice addictions registered nurse:

1. Derives and prioritizes diagnoses from the assessment data using appropriate complex clinical reasoning.

2. Formulates a differential diagnosis by systematically analyzing clinical and other related findings.

3. Makes diagnoses using advanced synthesis of information obtained during the interview, physical examination, mental status exam, diagnostic tests, or diagnostic procedures.

4. Bases differential diagnoses on criteria consistent with accepted classifications, such as current editions of *The Diagnostic and Statistical Manual of Mental Disorders IV-TR* (2000) and *The International Classification of Diseases 9 and 10* (1993).

The content in this appendix is not current and is of historical significance only.

STANDARD 3. OUTCOME IDENTIFICATION

The advanced practice registered nurse identifies expected outcomes derived from the assessment data and diagnoses, and individualizes expected outcomes with the patient and the healthcare team when appropriate.

Measurement Criteria

Expected outcomes are:

1. Identified with consideration of the associated risks, benefits, costs, availability and access.

2. Consistent with current theoretical, scientific, and clinical best practices knowledge.

3. Modified based on changes in the patient's healthcare status.

4. Identified with consideration of the entire wellness–illness addictions continuum.

5. Consistent with the patient's age, ethnicity, and socioeconomic and environmental circumstances.

STANDARD 4. PLANNING

The advanced practice addictions registered nurse develops a comprehensive treatment plan that includes interventions to attain expected outcomes.

Measurement Criteria

The comprehensive treatment plan:

1. Describes the assessment and diagnostic strategies and therapeutic interventions that reflect current addictions healthcare knowledge, theory, research, and practice.

2. Reflects the responsibilities of the advanced practice addictions registered nurse and the patient, and may include delegation of responsibilities to others.

3. Addresses strategies for promotion and restoration of health and prevention of illness, injury, and disease through independent clinical decision-making.

4. Is documented and modified to provide direction to other members of the healthcare team.

The content in this appendix is not current and is of historical significance only.

STANDARD 5. IMPLEMENTATION

The advanced practice addictions registered nurse prescribes, orders, or implements addictions interventions and treatments for the plan of care.

Measurement Criteria

The advanced practice addictions registered nurse:

1. Prescribes, performs, or implements interventions and treatments with knowledge of theory, research findings, and best practices.

2. Performs interventions and treatments within the scope of advanced practice addictions registered nursing.

STANDARD 5A. CASE MANAGEMENT AND COORDINATION OF CARE

The advanced practice addictions registered nurse provides comprehensive clinical coordination of care and case management.

Measurement Criteria

The advanced practice addictions registered nurse:

1. Provides case management and clinical coordination of care services using sophisticated data synthesis with consideration of the patient's complex needs and desired outcomes.

2. Negotiates health-related services and additional specialized care with the patient, appropriate systems, agencies, and providers.

The content in this appendix is not current and is of historical significance only.

STANDARD 5B. CONSULTATION

The advanced practice addictions registered nurse provides consultation to influence the plan of care for patients, enhance the abilities of others to provide quality care to addicted patients, and effect change in the system.

Measurement Criteria

1. Consultation activities are based on theory, research results, and best practices.

2. Consultation is based on mutual respect and defined role responsibility established with the patient.

3. Consultation recommendations are communicated in terms that facilitate understanding and involve the patient in decision-making.

4. The decision to implement the system change or plan of care remains the responsibility of the patient.

5. The decision to seek consultation is based on the patient's complex needs and the advance practice addictions registered nurse's recognition of need for additional expertise in managing patient care.

STANDARD 5C. HEALTH PROMOTION, HEALTH MAINTENANCE, AND HEALTH TEACHING

The advanced practice addictions registered nurse employs complex strategies, interventions, and teaching to promote, maintain, and improve health and prevent illness and injury.

Measurement Criteria

1. Health promotion and disease, illness, and injury prevention strategies are based on assessment of risks, learning theory, epidemiological principles, and the patient's health beliefs and practices.

2. Health promotion, maintenance, and teaching methods are appropriate to the patient's developmental level, learning needs, readiness and ability to learn, and culture.

The content in this appendix is not current and is of historical significance only.

STANDARD 5D. PRESCRIPTIVE AUTHORITY AND TREATMENT

The advanced practice addictions registered nurse uses prescriptive authority, procedures, and treatments in accordance with educational preparation, state and federal laws and regulations, applicable nurse practice acts, and appropriate advanced practice certification to treat illness and improve functional health status or to provide preventive care.

Measurement Criteria

The advanced practice addictions registered nurse:

1. Prescribes treatment interventions and procedures according to the patient's healthcare needs, based on current knowledge, practice, theory and research.

2. Performs procedures as needed in the delivery of comprehensive care.

3. Prescribes pharmacologic agents based on sound clinical decision-making using knowledge of pharmacological and physiological principles.

4. Prescribes specific pharmacologic agents or treatments based on clinical indicators or on the patient's status and needs, including the results of diagnostic and laboratory tests, as appropriate.

5. Monitors intended effects and potential adverse effects of pharmacologic and non-pharmacologic treatments, and adjusts them to promote optimal response in the patient.

6. Provides appropriate information about intended effects, potential adverse effects of the proposed prescription, costs, and alternative treatments and procedures to the patient.

The content in this appendix is not current and is of historical significance only.

STANDARD 5E. PSYCHOTHERAPY AND COMPLEMENTARY THERAPY

The advanced practice addictions registered nurse conducts individual, group, and family psychotherapy, and educates about and evaluates the use of complementary therapies to promote healthy lifestyles, prevent addictive behaviors, treat addictions and improve health status and functional abilities.

Measurement Criteria

1. Therapeutic modalities are individualized for the patient based on current theory, research, and best practices to prevent addiction and promote recovery.

2. Expected outcomes of psychotherapy are mutually determined based on patient need, and modified as necessary as recognized by both the patient and the advanced practice addiction registered nurse.

3. Theory, research, and the practice of complementary therapies are presented to the patient to ensure informed choices.

4. Complementary therapies are used by the advanced practice addictions registered nurse to promote health and well being of the patient, specifically when based on advanced training or certification.

STANDARD 5F. REFERRAL

The advanced practice addictions registered nurse identifies the need for additional care and makes referrals as needed.

Measurement Criteria

1. As a primary provider, the advanced practice addictions registered nurse facilitates continuity of care by implementing recommendations from referral sources.

2. The advanced practice addictions registered nurse refers directly to specific providers for additional care based upon patient needs, with consideration of benefits and costs.

The content in this appendix is not current and is of historical significance only.

STANDARD 6. EVALUATION

The advanced practice addictions registered nurse evaluates the patient's progress in attaining expected outcomes.

Measurement Criteria

1. The advanced practice addictions registered nurse evaluates the accuracy of diagnoses and effectiveness of interventions in relation to the patient's attainment of the expected outcomes.

2. The evaluation process is based on advanced knowledge, practice, theory and research, and results in revision or resolution of diagnoses, expected outcomes, and plan of care.

The content in this appendix is not current and is of historical significance only.

ADVANCED PRACTICE STANDARDS OF PROFESSIONAL PERFORMANCE FOR ADDICTIONS NURSING

STANDARD 7. QUALITY OF CARE

The advanced practice addictions registered nurse develops criteria for and evaluates the quality of care and effectiveness of advanced practice addictions registered nurses.

Measurement of Criteria

The advanced practice addictions registered nurse:

1. Assumes a leadership role as a clinical expert in establishing and monitoring standards of practice to improve care for patients with addictions.

2. Uses the results of quality of care activities to initiate changes throughout the healthcare system as appropriate.

3. Participates in efforts to facilitate timely treatment of the patient and minimize costs and unnecessary duplication of testing or other diagnostic activities.

4. Analyzes factors related to safety, satisfaction, effectiveness, and cost/benefit options with the patient, and other providers as appropriate.

5. Analyzes organizational systems for barriers to treatment, and promotes enhancements that affect patient healthcare status.

6. Bases the evaluation of care on current knowledge, practice, and research.

7. Seeks professional advanced practice certification in addictions nursing.

The content in this appendix is not current and is of historical significance only.

STANDARD 8. SELF-EVALUATION

The advanced practice addictions registered nurse continuously evaluates their nursing practice in relation to professional practice standards and relevant statutes and regulations, and is accountable to the public and to the profession for providing competent clinical care.

Measurement Criteria

The advanced practice addictions registered nurse:

1. Has the inherent responsibility as a professional to evaluate their performance according to the standards of the profession, and various regulatory bodies, and to take action to improve practice.

2. Seeks feedback regarding their practice and role performance from peers, professional colleagues, patients, and others.

3. Self-evaluates their practice based on patient outcomes.

STANDARD 9. EDUCATION

The advanced practice addictions registered nurse acquires and maintains current knowledge and skills in addictions practice.

Measurement Criteria

The advanced practice addictions registered nurse:

1. Uses current healthcare research to expand clinical knowledge, enhance role performance, and increase knowledge of professional issues.

2. Seeks experiences and formal and independent learning activities to maintain and develop clinical and professional skills and knowledge.

The content in this appendix is not current and is of historical significance only.

STANDARD 10. LEADERSHIP

The advanced practice addictions registered nurse serves as a leader and a role model for the professional development of peers, colleagues, and others.

Measurement Criteria

The advanced practice addictions registered nurse:

1. Contributes to the professional development of others to improve patient care and to foster the profession's growth.

2. Brings creativity and innovation to nursing practice to improve care delivery.

3. Participates in professional nursing organization activities.

4. Works to influence policy-making bodies to improve patient care and promote access to care.

STANDARD 11. ETHICS

The advanced practice addictions registered nurse integrates ethical principles and norms in all areas of practice.

Measurement Criteria

The advanced practice addictions registered nurse:

1. Maintains a therapeutic and professional relationship and discusses the delineation of roles and parameters of the relationship with the patient.

2. Informs the patient of the risks, benefits, and outcomes of healthcare regimens.

3. Contributes to resolving the ethical problems or dilemmas of individuals or systems.

The content in this appendix is not current and is of historical significance only.

Standard 12. Interdisciplinary Process

The advanced practice addictions registered nurse promotes an interdisciplinary process in providing patient care.

Measurement Criteria

The advanced practice addictions registered nurse:

1. Works with other disciplines to enhance patient care via interdisciplinary activities, which may include education, consultation, management, technological development or research opportunities.

2. Facilitates an interdisciplinary process with other members of the healthcare team in implementing the plan of care.

Standard 13. Research

The advanced practice addictions registered nurse utilizes theory and research to discover, examine, and evaluate knowledge, theories, and creative approaches to healthcare practice.

Measurement Criteria

The advanced practice addictions registered nurse:

1. Critically evaluates practice in light of past and current research findings disseminated by the National Institutes of Health (NIAAA and NIDA), professional journals such as *Journal of Addictions Nursing*, and other sources.

2. Identifies relevant research questions in practice related to addiction.

3. Participates in related research as available.

4. Disseminates relevant research findings through practice, education, publication, or consultation.

The content in this appendix is not current and is of historical significance only.

GLOSSARY

Abuse. A maladaptive pattern of substance use. (See *Substance abuse.*)

Addiction. A complex neurobiobehavioral disorder characterized by impaired control, compulsive use, dependency, and craving for the activity, substance, or food. Relapses are possible even after long periods of abstinence (National Institute on Drug Abuse [NIDA], 2002b; Wilcox & Erickson, 2000). Addiction is often (but not always) accompanied by physiological dependence, consisting of a withdrawal syndrome, or tolerance (NIDA, 2002a). Factors contributing to the development of addiction include genetic predisposition, the reinforcing properties and access to the substance, food or activity, family and peer influences, sociocultural environment, personality, and existing psychiatric disorders (Goldstein, 1994). The terms addictive disorder and addiction are used interchangeably.

At-risk use. The occasional abuse of substances without yet experiencing negative consequences of substance abuse (Adapted from CSAT: SAMHSA, 1997).

Co-occurring disorder. The concurrent presence of two or more independent (but invariably interactive) disorders/conditions, such as substance abuse, physical illness, mental retardation, or mental illness (CSAT: SAMHSA, 1994).

Craving. The conscious awareness of the desire to take a drug. It is a complex neurobiobehavioral phenomenon based on previous experiences with addictive substances or activities (Goldstein, 1994; Ruden and Byalick, 1997; Drummond, 2001).

Dependency. Synonymous with addiction. (See *Addiction; Substance dependence.*)

Detoxification. Preventing or reducing the symptoms of withdrawal from alcohol or other drugs with the goal of "normalization of the person's body chemistry, primarily the neurochemistry, so that the individual is able to function in a manner similar to that experienced prior to the consumption of the substance" (Feigenbaum & Allen, 1996, p. 142).

Eating disorders. Neurobiobehavioral disorders characterized by the inability to regulate eating habits and frequent tendency to overuse or underuse food that interferes with biological, psychological, and sociocultural integrity. Illnesses associated with maladaptive eating regulation responses include anorexia nervosa, bulimia nervosa, and binge eating disorder (Cochrane, 2001, p. 527; American Psychiatric Association [APA], 2000; CSAT: SAMHSA, 1997).

The content in this appendix is not current and is of historical significance only.

Harm/risk reduction. The "application of methods designed to reduce harm (and risk of harm) associated with ongoing or active addictive behaviors" (Marlatt & Tapert, 1993; Marlatt . & Witkiewitz, 2002).

Impulse-control disorder. Failure to resist an impulse, drive, or temptation to perform an act that is harmful to the person or to others (Blum et al, 1996, Blum et al, 2000; Nestler, 2001; Roberts & Koob, 1997). One example is *pathological gambling* characterized by persistent and recurrent maladaptive gambling behavior that disrupts personal, family, or vocational pursuits (Adapted from APA, 2000, p. 671).

Low risk use. Consumption of small amounts of substances infrequently and not in high-risk situations (Adapted from CSAT: SAMHSA, 1997).

Physiological dependence. A state of adaptation to a substance manifested by tolerance or withdrawal (APA, 2000; NIDA, 2002a).

Prevention. Health care activities aimed at persons who currently do not have the disease or are in the early stages of the disease, rather than the treatment of disease. Prevention activities include reduction of risk, promotion of health behaviors that prevent occurrences of disease and reduce harm (Marlatt & Witkiewitz, 2002), and early detection and treatment to prevent the development of additional consequences of the disease (Ervin, 2002).

Relapse. A recurrence of problem substance use or activity in someone who was abstinent from that substance use or activity (Trachtenberg & Fleming, 1994). It is considered a "normal part of the cycle of change" (Velasquez, Mauer, Crouch & DiClemente, 2001, p. 189) in the recovery from addiction, which involves experiencing a "slip" and reverting to exhibiting the addictive behavior.

Remission. The state in which a person is free of symptoms of substance dependence, substance abuse, impulse disorder, or eating disorder.

Substance abuse. A maladaptive pattern of substance use (i.e., problem use) within the previous 12 months, leading to clinically significant impairment or distress as manifested by repeated occurrence of one or more of the following: (1) failure to fulfill major role obligations, (2) use in physically hazardous situations, (3) legal problems, and (4) continued use despite consequences resulting from use. (Adapted from APA, 2000.)

The content in this appendix is not current and is of historical significance only.

REFERENCES

Adlaf, E. M. & Ialomiteanu, A. (2000). Prevalence of problem gambling in adolescents: Findings from the 1999 Ontario student drug use survey. *Canadian Journal of Psychiatry*, 45 (8) 752–755.

Allen, K., ed. (1996). *Nursing Care of the Addicted Client*. Philadelphia: Lippincott.

American Nurses Association (1984). *Addictions and psychological dysfunction in nursing: The profession's response to the problem*. Kansas City, MO: American Nurses Association.

American Nurses Association, National Nurses Society on Addictions, & Drug and Alcohol Nurses Association (1987). *Care of clients with addictions: Dimensions of nursing practice*. Kansas City, MO: American Nurses Association.

American Nurses Association. (1996). *Scope and Standards of Advanced Practice Registered Nursing*. Washington, DC: American Nurses Publishing.

American Nurses Association. (1998). *Scope and Standards of Clinical Nursing Practice, Second Edition*. Washington, DC: American Nurses Publishing.

American Psychiatric Association. (2000) *Diagnostic and statistical manual, 4th ed., text revision*. Washington, DC: American Psychiatric Association.

Armstrong, M., Feigenbaum, J., Savage, C., Snow, D., & Vourakis, C., eds. (2005). *Core curriculum of addictions nursing, 2nd edition*. Raleigh, NC: International Nurses Society on Addiction.

Blum, K., Braverman, E. R., Holder, J. M., Lubar, J. F., Monastra, V. J., Miller, D., Lubar, J. O., Chen, T. J., & Comings, D. E. (2000). Reward deficiency syndrome: A biogenetic model for the diagnosis and treatment of impulsive, addictive, and compulsive behaviors. *Journal of Psychoactive Drugs*, 32 (Supplement), i–iv, 1–112.

Blum, K., Cull, J. G., Braverman, E. R., & Comings, D. E. (1996). Reward deficiency syndrome. *American Scientist*, 84, 132–145.

Blume, S. (1997). Pathological gambling. In *Substance abuse: a comprehensive textbook, 3rd ed.*, Lowinson, J.; Ruiz, P.; Millman, R.; & Langrod, J., 330–337. Baltimore: Williams & Wilkins.

Blundell, J.E. & Hill, A.J. (1993). Binge eating: Psychobiological mechanisms. In *Binge eating—Nature, assessment, and treatment*, Fairburn, C.G. & Wilson, G.T., eds., 206–224. New York: Guilford Press.

The content in this appendix is not current and is of historical significance only.

Booth, J. & Martin, J.E. (1998). Spiritual and religious factors in substance use, dependence and recovery. In *Handbook of religious & mental health*, Koenig, H.G., ed. 175–200. New York: NY: Academic Press.

Buckner, M. (2002). *Substance abuse among nursing students. Dean's notes: A communication service to nursing school deans, administrators, and faculty.* Anthony J. Jannetti, Inc.

Burns, E., Thompson. ,A. & Ciccone, J. (1991). *An addictions curriculum for nurses and other helping professionals.* Columbus, OH: Ohio State University.

CSAT: SAMHSA (Center for Substance Abuse Treatment. Substance Abuse and Mental Health Service Administration). (1999). *Enhancing motivation for change in substance abuse treatment: Treatment Improvement Protocol (TIP).* Series 35. Washington, DC: Department of Health and Human Services publication No. (SMA) 99-3354.

CSAT/SAHMSA (Center for Substance Abuse Treatment. Substance Abuse and Mental Health Services Administration.) (1997). *A guide to substance abuse services for primary care clinicians: Treatment improvement protocol (TIP).* Series 24. Washington, DC: Department of Health and Human Services publication No. (SMA) 97-3139, 1–23.

CSAT/SAHMSA (Center for Substance Abuse Treatment. Substance Abuse and Mental Health Services Administration.) (1994). *Assessment and treatment of patients with coexisting mental illness and alcohol and other drug abuse. (TIP).* Series 9. Washington, DC: Department of Health and Human Services publication No. (SMA) 94-2078, 3–7.

CSAT/SAHMSA (Center for Substance Abuse Prevention. Substance Abuse and Mental Health Services Administration.) (1994) *Nurse training course: Prevention of alcohol, tobacco, and other drug problems.* Rockville, MD: U.S. Department of Health and Human Services. Substance Abuse and Mental Health Services Administration.

Cochrane, C. E. (2001). Eating regulation responses and eating disorders. In *Principles and practices of psychiatric nursing (7th ed.)*, Stuart, G.W. & Laraia, M.T., eds., 526–547. St. Louis: C. V. Mosby.

Compton, M. (1996). Research in addictions nursing. In *Nursing care of the addicted client,* Allen, K.M., ed., 304–330. Philadelphia: Lippincott.

Davis, C. & Claridge, G. (1998). The eating disorders as addiction: A psychobiological perspective. *Addictive Behaviors*, 23: 463–475.

Drummond, D.C. (2001), Theories of drug craving, ancient and modern. *Addiction,* 96:33–46.

The content in this appendix is not current and is of historical significance only.

Dyehouse, Janice M. & Sommers, Marilyn Sawyer. (1998). Brief intervention after alcohol-related injuries. *Nursing clinics of North America*, Vol. 33(1): 93–104.

Ervin, N.E. (2002). *Advanced Community Health Nursing Practice.* Saddle River, New Jersey: Prentice Hall.

Feigenbaum, J. C. & Allen, K. M. (1996). Detoxification. In *Nursing care of the addicted client*, Allen, K.M., ed., 139–176. Philadelphia: Lippincott.

Finnell, D. (2002) *Certification in addictions nursing: Promoting and protecting the health of the public*. A white paper. Raleigh, NC: Addictions Nursing Certification Board & International Nurses Society on Addiction.

Gerace, L., Sullivan, E. J., Murphy, S. & Cotter, F. (1992). Faculty development and curriculum change in alcohol and other drug abuse. *Nurse Educator*, 17(1), 24–27.

Gold, M.; Johnson, C.; & Stennie, K. (1997). Eating disorders. In *Substance abuse: A comprehensive textbook, 3rd ed.*, Lowinson, J., Ruiz, P., Millman, R. & Langrod, J., eds., 319–330. Baltimore: Williams & Wilkins.

Goldstein A. (1994). *Addiction: From biology to drug policy*. New York: WH Freeman.

Goodman, A. (1997). Sexual addiction. In *Substance abuse: A comprehensive textbook, 3rd ed.*, Lowinson, J., Ruiz, P., Millman, R. & Langrod, J., eds., 340–354. Baltimore: Williams & Wilkins.

Haack, M. R. & Adger H. (2002) Strategic plan for interdisciplinary faculty development. *Substance Abuse* 23 (3S), 345.

Hagemaster, J. N., Plumlee, A., Connors, H. & Sullivan, E. J. (1994). Integration of substance abuse content into undergraduate and graduate curricula. *Journal of Alcohol and Drug Education*, 40(1), 26–30.

Hall, M.J. & Popovich, J.R. (2000). *Summary: National hospital discharge summary advance data from vital and health statistics. no. 316*. Hyattsville, MD: National Center for Health Statistics.

Happell, B. & Taylor, C. (1999). Drug and alcohol education for nurses: have we examined the whole problem? *Journal of Addictions Nursing*, 11(4), 180–185.

Hoffman, A. L. & Heinemann, M. E. (1987). Substance abuse education in schools of nursing: A national survey. *Journal of Nursing Education*, 26(70), 282–287.

Huebner, H. (1993). *Endorphins, eating disorders, and other addictive behaviors*. New York: W. W. Norton.

The content in this appendix is not current and is of historical significance only.

Jacobs, D. F. (2000). Juvenile gambling in North America: An analysis of long term trends and future prospects. *Journal of Gambling Studies,* 16(2/3), 119–152.

Johnston, L. D., O'Malley, P. M., & Bachman, J. G. (2003). *Monitoring the future—National results on adolescent drug use: Overview of key findings, 2002.* NIH Publication No. 03-5374. Bethesda, MD: National Institute on Drug Abuse.

Korper, S. P., & Council, C. L. (Eds.). (2002). *Substance use by older adults: Estimates of future impact on the treatment systems* (DHHS Publication No. SMA 03-3763, Analytic Series A-21). Rockville, MD: Substance Abuse and Mental Health Services Administration, Office of Applied Studies.

Marcus, M.T. (1997). Faculty development and curricular change: A process and outcomes model for substance abuse education. *Journal of Professional Nursing,* 13:3, 168–177.

Marlatt, G. A. & Tapert. S.F. (1993). Harm reduction: Reducing the risks of addictive behaviors. In *Addictive behaviors across the life span: Prevention, treatment, and policy issues,* Baer, J.S., Marlatt, G.A. & McMahon, R.J., eds., 243–273. Newbury Park: CA: Sage.

Marlatt, G. A., & Witkiewitz, K. (2002). Harm reduction approaches to alcohol use: Health promotion, prevention, and treatment. *Addictive Behaviors, 27,* 867–886.

Martinez R. & Murphy-Parker, D.M. (2003). Examining the relationship of addiction education and beliefs of nursing students toward persons with alcohol problems. *Archives of Psychiatric Nursing,* 17:4, 156–164.

McRee, B., Babor, T. & Church, O. (1991). *Project NEADA (Nursing education in alcohol and drug abuse).* University of Connecticut School of Nursing.

Mertens, I.L. & Van Gaal, L. (2000). Promising new approaches to the management of obesity. *Drugs,* 60 (1), 1–9.

Murphy-Parker, D. Kronenbitter, S. & Kronenbitter, R. (2003). National Student Nurses Association passes resolution in support of nursing school policies to assist and advocate nursing students experiencing impaired practice. *The Drug and Alcohol Professional,* 3 (2), 9–14.

Murray, C.J. & Lopez, A.D., eds. (1996*).* The global burden of disease. A comprehensive assessment of mortality and disability from diseases, injuries and risk factors in 1990 and projected to 2020. *Global Burden of Disease and Injury, Vol. 1.* Cambridge: Harvard University Press.

Naegle, M. & D'Areangelo, J. (1991). *Project SAEN (Substance Abuse Education in Nursing).* New York: New York University Division of Nursing.

The content in this appendix is not current and is of historical significance only.

National Gambling Impact and Policy Commission (NGIPC). (1999). *Final report—The national gambling impact study.* Washington, DC: NGIPC.

National Institute on Alcohol Abuse and Alcoholism. (1998). Drug abuse cost to society set at $97.7 billion, continuing steady increase since 1975. *NIDA Notes,* 13 (4), 1, 12–13.

National Institute on Drug Abuse (NIDA) (2002a). *Diagnosis and treatment of drug abuse in family practice.* Public Health Service, National Institutes of Health (NIH), Department of Health and Human Services (DHHS), http://165.112.78.61/Diagnosis-Treatment/Diagnosis2.html, (accessed November 20, 2002).

National Institute on Drug Abuse (NIDA) (2002b). [Last updated September 13, 2002]. *Frequently asked questions:* What is drug addiction? Public Health Service, National Institutes of Health (NIH), Department of Health and Human Services (DHHS), http://www.drugabuse.gov/tools/FAQ.html, (accessed November 3, 2002).

National Nurses Society on Addiction (1993). Position paper: Addictive disorders among nurses and nursing students in academic settings. *Perspectives in Addictions Nursing,* 4(3), 1, 7–8.

National Nurses Society on Addiction & American Nurses Association. (1989). *Standards of addiction nursing practice with selected diagnoses and criteria.* Kansas City, MO: American Nurses Association.

Nestler, E. J. (2001). Molecular neurobiology of addiction. *American Journal on Addictions,* 10, 201–217.

Pace, E. (2002). The employee assistance program as a model of care for an addicted colleague: Peer assistance, by nurses for nurses. *The Drug and Alcohol Professional,* 2 (3), 41–47.

Petrakis, I., & Krystal, J. (1997). Neuroscience: Implications for treatment. *Alcohol Health & Research World,* 21(2), 157–160.

Pirke, K. M. (1990). Central neurotransmitter disturbances in bulimia (nervosa). In *Bulimia nervosa: basic research, diagnosis and therapy,* Fichter, M. M., ed., 223–233. New York: John Wiley & Sons.

Rassool, G. H. (Ed.) (1998). *Substance use and misuse: Nature, context and clinical interventions.* Oxford: Blackwell Science.

Rassool, G. (2002). Substance misuse and mental health: An overview. *Nursing Standard,* 16 (50), 46–52.

The content in this appendix is not current and is of historical significance only.

Reisman, B.L. & Shrader, R.W. (1984). Effect of nurses' attitudes toward alcoholism on their referral rate for treatment. *Occupational Health Nursing* 32, 273–275.

Roberts, A. J., & Koob, G. F. (1997). The Neurobiology of addiction—An overview. *Alcohol Health & Research World*, 21(2), 101–108.

Ruden, R. A & Byalick, M. (1997) *The craving brain*. New York: HarperCollins.

Shaffer, H.J. & Hall, M.N. (2001). Updating and refining prevalence estimates of disordered gambling behavior in the United States and Canada. *Canadian Journal of Public Health*, 92(3), 168–172.

Sheehan, A. (1992). Nurses respond to substance abuse. *International Nurses Review*, 39(5), 141–144.

Smith, G.B. (1992). Attitudes of nurse managers and assistant nurse managers toward chemically impaired colleagues. *Image: Journal of Nursing Scholarship*, 24, 295–300.

Snow, D. (2000a) Managing patients with alcohol use disorders. *Lippincott's Primary Care Practice*, 4 (2), 131–148.

Snow, D (2000b) Neurobiology of addiction: The time has come. *Journal of Addictions Nursing*, 13 (3 &4), 3–4.

Starkey, P. J. (1980). Nurses' attitudes toward alcoholism. *AORN*, 31, 822.

Subcommittee on Health Services Research, National Advisory Council on Alcohol Abuse and Alcoholism. *Improving the delivery of alcohol treatment and prevention services: A national plan for alcohol health services research* (1997). Publication N. 97-4223. Bethesda, MD: National Institute on Alcohol Abuse and Alcoholism, National Institutes of Health, Department of Health and Human Services.

Substance Abuse and Mental Health Services Administration (SAMHSA). (2002). *Results from the 2001 National Household Survey on Drug Abuse: Volume I. Summary of national findings*. Office of Applied Studies, NHSDA Series H-17, DHHS Publication No. SMA 02-3758. Rockville, MD.

Sullivan, E. J. (1995). *Nursing care of clients with substance abuse*. St. Louis: Mosby.

Sullivan, E. J. & Handley, S. M. (1993). Nursing research on alcohol and drug abuse. In *Annual Review of Nursing Research. Vol.11*, Fitzpatrick, J.J., Taunton, R.L., & Benoliel, J.O., eds. New York: Springer.

Sullivan, E.F, & Fleming, M. (1997). A guide to substance abuse services for primary care clinicians. Treatment Improvement Protocol (TIP) Series 24.

The content in this appendix is not current and is of historical significance only.

Tamlyn, D.L. (1989). The effect of education on student nurses' attitudes toward alcoholics. *Canadian Journal of Nursing Research*, 21(3), 31–47.

Teutsch, S. (1992). A framework for assessing the effectiveness of disease and injury prevention. *Morbidity and Mortality Weekly Report*, 41 (RR-3), 1–12.

Trachtenberg, A. I., & Fleming, M. F. (1994). *Diagnosis and treatment of drug abuse in family practice.* Rockville, MD: National Institute of Drug Abuse.

Trinkoff, A.M., Eaton, W.W. & Anthony, J.C. (1991). The Prevalence of Substance Abuse Among Registered Nurses. *Nursing Research*, 40 (3), 172–75.

U.S. DHHS (Department of Health and Human Services). (2000). *Healthy People 2010*. National Center for Health Statistics. Hyattsville, MD: NCHS.

Velasquez, M. M.., Mauer, G. G., Crouch, C., & DiClemente, C. C. (2001). *Group treatment for substance abuse—A stages-of-change-therapy manual*. New York: Guilford Press.

Volberg, R.A. (1994). The prevalence and demographics of pathological gamblers: implications for public health: *American Journal of Public Health*, 84 (2), 237–41.

Vourakis, C. (1996). Addictions nursing practice is knowledge specific. *Journal of Addictions Nursing*, 8 (1), 2–3.

Wilcox, R.E. & Erickson, C.K. (2000). Neurological aspects of addictions. *Journal of Addictions Nursing*, 12 (3/4), 117–132.

Winick, C. (1997). Epidemiology. In *Substance abuse: A comprehensive textbook*. 3rd.ed., Lowinson, J., Ruiz, P., Millman, R. & Langrod, J., 10–16. Baltimore: Williams & Wilkins.

World Health Organization (1992). *The ICD-9. Classification of mental and behavioral disorders: Diagnostic criteria for research*. Geneva: World Health Organization.

World Health Organization (1993). *The ICD-10. Classification of mental and behavioral disorders: Diagnostic criteria for research*. Geneva: World Health Organization.

The content in this appendix is not current and is of historical significance only.

APPENDIX A
Specific Prevention Strategies

Information dissemination provides awareness and knowledge of the nature and extent of addictive behaviors, and their effects on persons, families, and communities. It also provides information to increase perception of risk, and information on healthy lifestyles.

Development of life coping skills seeks to affect critical life and social skills. Some of these include:

- decision-making,
- refusal,
- critical analysis,
- communication techniques,
- goal-setting,
- values clarification,
- problem-solving techniques,
- self-responsibility and self-care, and
- stress management and relaxation techniques.

Provision of alternatives involves targeted populations in activities that exclude addictive behaviors.

Community development aims to enhance the ability of the community to provide prevention and treatment services.

Advocacy for a healthy environment is used to set up or change written community standards, codes, and attitudes that influence and contribute to addiction.

Problem identification actually refers to secondary prevention, and involves screening and referral. After identification, this strategy calls for education and counseling of those who show evidence of being at risk for developing an addiction, and focusing on harm reduction strategies to prevent the development of additional problems related to addictions.

Primary prevention is utilized during the experimental/social stage of the process of addiction. Problem identification and other interventions are utilized during the problem use/abuse stage of the addictions process.

The content in this appendix is not current and is of historical significance only.

APPENDIX B
Motivational Interventions

According to CSAT:SAMHSA (1997) motivation is a key to change, multidimensional, a dynamic and fluctuating state, interactive, and influenced by the clinician's style.

In motivating a patient to change, the following strategies are recommended:

- Focus on the patient's strengths rather than their weaknesses.
- Respect the patient's autonomy and decisions.
- Provide individualized and patient-centered care.
- Do not depersonalize the patient by using labels like "addict".
- Develop a therapeutic partnership.
- Use empathy rather than authority or power.
- Focus on early intervention.
- Understand that intervention can happen in any setting.
- Recognize that addiction exists along a continuum.
- Recognize that many patients have more than one addiction.
- Recognize that many patients have other coexisting psychiatric or medical disorders that affect all stages of the change process.
- Accept goals that incorporate harm reduction, interim, incremental, and even temporary steps toward the ultimate goal of abstinence.
- Integrate interventions work with work done by other disciplines.

A motivational intervention is any clinical strategy designed to enhance patient motivation for change. It can include counseling, patient assessment, multiple sessions, or a 30-minute brief intervention.

The content in this appendix is not current and is of historical significance only.

The following elements of current motivational approaches have been found to be critical in prompting a person to change (SAMHSA, 1999b):

1) Use the FRAMES approach.

2) Incorporate decisional balance exercises.

3) Develop discrepancies for patients.

4) Use flexible pacing.

5) Establish personal contact with patients who are not actively in treatment.

The FRAMES approach consists of:

Feedback regarding personal risk or impairment following an assessment .

Responsibility for the change being placed with the patient.

Advice about changing—reducing or stopping the addictive behavior—given in a nonjudgmental manner.

Menu of self-directed change options and treatment alternatives offered to the patient.

Empathic counseling showing warmth, respect, and understanding.

Self-efficacy or optimistic empowerment engendered in the person to encourage change.

Research has shown that simple motivational interventions can be effective in encouraging patients to change, comply with treatment, or even return for more clinical appointments. Motivational interventions can take place in any setting, and offer great potential to reach persons with differing types of addictions from different cultural groups (CSAT:SAMHSA, 1997).

One of the key brief intervention activities is screening. Screening is usually done using brief written, oral, or computerized questionnaires. No screening instrument is effective with all persons. Therefore, it is important to consider a person's age, gender, race, ethnicity, and addiction before deciding on what screening instrument to use.

Screenings take approximately 10 to 15 minutes and are completed for the purposes of determining if a patient needs to be referred for a more in-depth assessment. Once the above considerations have been determined, it is important to use a screening instrument that has proven reliability and validity with the group of which the patient to be screened is a member. Many screening instruments exist that meet these criteria. They are easy to obtain in the literature, from books, or from addictions-related government clearinghouses.

The content in this appendix is not current and is of historical significance only.

APPENDIX C
Code of Ethics for Addictions Nurses

This code of ethics guides addictions nurses in maintaining a high level of competency in the provision of addictions nursing services.

As an addictions nurse, I acknowledge that my primary responsibility, regardless of any specific job title, is to meet my nursing responsibilities to the best of my ability. In implementing my responsibilities, I will adhere to the following principles:

I will remember that the care of the client is primary and I will ensure that he or she receives the highest possible level of quality care.

I will adhere to professional nursing standards and addictions nursing standards as currently defined.

I will understand and abide by the principles contained in the American Nurses Association Code for Nurses.

I will observe and maintain all rules of confidentiality.

I will conduct myself in such a professional manner as to promote the best interests of my clients and co-workers.

I will strive to increase my professional knowledge through continuing education.

I will seek and use professional supervision as a means of ensuring my competence to provide high quality care.

I will respect the boundaries of therapeutic relationships, and will not initiate or be the recipient of any personal or business relationships with clients.

I will strive to maintain my own personal health, so that I am fully capable of meeting my professional responsibilities, and will promptly seek assistance for any health problems or needs.

I will advocate on behalf of colleagues and nurses whose practice has become impaired as a result of addiction and/or psychological dysfunction, to ensure that they are treated fairly and appropriately.

The content in this appendix is not current and is of historical significance only.

I will respect the dignity and rights of all others, and will not discriminate against any client on the basis of race, gender, age, ethnicity, or religion.

I will act as an advocate for high quality addictions prevention and treatment within my workplace and my community.

I will recognize that the prevention of addictions is possible and I will engage in prevention activities within my worksite and my community.

~~~~

Published originally by National Nurses Society on Addictions (1995). Reprinted with permission of International Nurses Society on Addictions.

Appendix B.

The Savage and Finnell Conceptual Model

This is a larger version of the illustration of the Savage and Finnell Conceptual Model of the Continuum of Substance Use and Maladaptive Behaviors: Nursing Foci© on pg. 9 and as discussed on pgs 8 and 9. Please cite the page 9 instance.

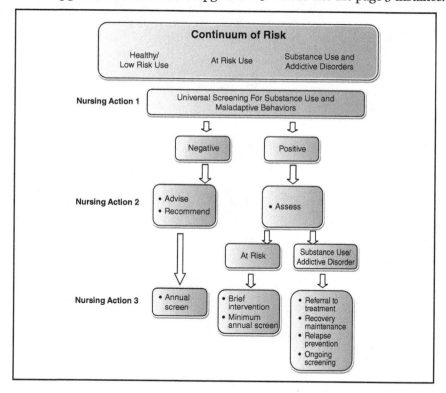

Legend: Substance use (alcohol, tobacco, and other drugs) and behaviors that are maladaptive can progress to substance use and addictive disorders.

- The *level of risk* is identified by using established screening tools. Individuals with detectable risk are further assessed for clinically significant impairment or distress. (The gradual shading in the figure conveys the progression from healthy risk or low risk to at-risk to a diagnosable disorder.)
- *Nursing actions* are tailored according to the level or risk and in accord with guidelines for brief intervention and referral to treatment. Taking the level of risk into account, the overarching clinical outcomes focus on reducing risk associated with substance use and maladaptive behaviors. Across all levels of risk, nurses engage in patient-centered discussions to negotiate goals fostering optimal clinical outcomes.
- Recognizing that substance use and maladaptive behaviors are not static, screening is repeated during subsequent encounters in accord with the individual's risk level.

Index

Note: Entries with [2004] indicate content from *Scope and Standards of Addictions Nursing Practice* (2004), reproduced in Appendix A. That information is not current but included for historical value only.

A

referral, 107, 164
See also Standard of Care for
Addictions Nursing [2004]

Advanced Practice Standards of
Professional Performance for
Addictions Nursing [2004]
education, 108, 167
ethics, 108, 168
interdisciplinary process, 108, 169
leadership, 108, 168
quality of care, 108, 166
research, 108, 169
self-evaluation, 108, 167
See also Standard of Professional
Performance for Addictions
Nursing

Advise and assist brief interventions, 8–9
See also Intervention

Advocacy in addictions nursing practice,
1, 5, 25, 35–36

Affordable Care Act (ACA), 29

Alcohol use, 2, 6, 7, 10, 11, 12, 33, 34, 121
at-risk, 29, 33, 38
in nurses, 136
pregnancy and, 39
screening for, 7, 8
standard drink, 10

Alcoholics Anonymous (AA), 23

American Association of Addiction
Psychiatry (AAAP), 32

American Nurses Association (ANA), 1, 2
documents, 2

American Psychiatric Association, 11

American Society for Pain Management
Nursing (ASPMN), 31, 36

American Society of Addiction Medicine
(ASAM), 32

ANA. *See* American Nurses Association
(ANA)

Analysis. *See* Critical thinking

ANCB. *See* Addictions Nursing
Certification Board (ANCB)

ANSA. *See* Association of Nurses in
Substance Abuse (ANSA)

APRNs. *See* Advanced practice registered
nurses (APRNs) in addictions nursing
practice

ASAM. *See* American Society of
Addiction Medicine (ASAM)

Ask, Advise, Assess, Assist, Arrange
follow-up in SBIRT, 7

ASPMN. *See* American Society for Pain
Management Nursing (ASPMN)

Assessment in addictions nursing
practice 5, 11, 33
Advanced Practice Standard of Care
[2004], 107, 159
assessment data, 48, 60
competencies involving, 46–47, 48,
52, 60
pain assessment and management, 36
risk assessment and management,
27, 31
Standard of Care [2004], 105,
138–139
measurement criteria, 138
Standard of Practice, 46–47
substance-specific, 37

Association of Nurses in Substance
Abuse (ANSA), 20

At risk activities and individuals, 5, 11,
13, 14
alcohol use, 29, 33, 38
at-risk population, 10–11
at-risk use defined, 170

Attitudes in addictions nursing practice,
1, 24, 26, 117
See also Values, attitudes, and beliefs

Awareness in addictions nursing practice,
7, 8, 26, 36
self-awareness, 129

B

Baccalaureate nursing programs, 15

Benefits and cost. *See* Cost and economic
controls

Biopsychosocial model, 115

Drug use, 1, 6, 7, 8, 19, 114, 121, 136, 147
  molecular adaptations and, 114
  in nurses, 136
  screening for, 7, 8
DrugFree.org, 10

E

Eating disorders, 2
  defined, 170
  See also Food addiction
Economic controls. *See* Cost and
  economic controls
Education in addictions nursing practice,
  27, 40, 133–134
  addictions nurses, 15, 19
  Advanced Practice Standard of
    Professional Performance [2004],
    108, 167
  competencies involving. 56, 57, 59,
    64–65, 66, 70, 72
  healthcare consumers, 57
  Standard of Professional
    Performance, 64–65
    [2004], 106, 153
Emergency nurses, 34–35
Environment in addictions nursing
  practice, 27
  See also Practice environments and
    settings
Environmental health in addictions
  nursing practice
  competencies involving, 77–78
  Standard of Professional
    Performance, 77–78
Ethics in addictions nursing practice,
  24–28
  Advanced Practice Standard of
    Professional Performance [2004],
    108, 168
  code of ethics for addictions nurses
    [2004], 182–183
  competencies involving, 47, 49,
    62–63, 67
  peer assistance for nurses and, 36

Standard of Care [2004], 108
Standard of Professional
  Performance, 62–63
  [2004], 106, 155
Etiology, addiction, 115
Evaluation in addictions nursing practice,
  36, 38
  Advanced Practice Standard of Care
    [2004], 107, 165
  competencies involving, 49, 56, 57, 59,
    60–61, 67, 68, 75, 76
  Standard of Care [2004], 105, 150
    measurement criteria, 150
  Standard of Practice, 60–61
  See also Professional practice
    evaluation
Evidence-based interventions in
  addictions nursing practice, 13, 32–33
Evidence-based practice and research in
  addictions nursing practice
  competencies involving, 66
  Standard of Professional
    Performance, 66
Excellence in addictions nursing practice,
  22

F

Families in addictions nursing practice,
  43, 46, 62, 72, 73, 75, 107, 117, 121,
  128, 129, 130, 134, 135
  addictions phenomena of concern on,
    126
  history, 138
  psychotherapy, 107, 164
  See also Healthcare consumers
FDA. *See* Food and Drug Administration
  (FDA)
Financial issues. *See* Cost and economic
  controls
5 As, SBIRT, 7
Follow-up care in addictions nursing
  practice, 7, 30, 38
Food addiction, 113, 114, 170

Addictions Nursing: Scope and Standards of Practice

Addictions Nursing: Scope and Standards of Practice